DO YOU KNOW ANYONE IN THE UNDERGROUND ECONOMY?

He may be a doctor, collecting his fees in cash only.

Or a waiter, not reporting tips.

Or a businessman, using two cash registers to ring up sales.

Or an investor, buying bearer bonds that the IRS cannot trace.

Or the one and only member of a so-called "church."

He may be acting legally—or illegally.

Whoever he is and whatever he's doing, the money he's saving and the risks he's taking—you'll find out all about it in the book that tells you everything the IRS might not want you to know.

INSIDE THE
UNDERGROUND ECONOMY

Recommended MENTOR and SIGNET Books

☐ **THE AFFLUENT SOCIETY by John Kenneth Galbraith.** Third Revised Edition. The book that added a new phrase to our language, a new classic to literature, and changed the basic economic attitudes of our age. In this new revision, Galbraith has extensively updated the information and widened the perspectives of his basic argument ... "Daring ... a compelling challenge to conventional thought." —*The New York Times* (#ME1894—$2.95)

☐ **THE NEW INDUSTRIAL STATE by John Kenneth Galbraith.** Third Revised Edition. One of our most distinguished economists and author of such bestsellers as *The Affluent Society* offers a comprehensive look at modern economic life and the changes that are shaping its future. (#ME1764—$3.50)

☐ **UNDERSTANDING THE ECONOMY: For People Who Can't Stand Economics by Alfred L. Malabre, Jr.** The U.S. economic scene made easily comprehensible and intensely interesting ... "Millions of readers can learn from this lively book."—Paul Samuelson, Nobel Prize-winning economist. (#MJ1800—$1.95)

☐ **UNDERSTANDING FINANCIAL STATEMENTS by John Myer.** A handbook for executives, students and investors presenting samples of each type of accounting statement with full explanation of how the figures may be interpreted and used. Illustrated. Index. (#ME1855—$2.25)

☐ **TAX SHELTERS. A Complete Guide by Robert and Carol Tannenhauser.** In simple, concise language, a top lawyer explains the latest legislation and rulings and tells you which shelters work and which are outmoded. Cash-flow charts plot savings through 1989, and a glossary turns technical terms and IRS-ese into plain English. (#AE1046—$2.75)

INSIDE THE
UNDERGROUND
ECONOMY

by Jerome Tuccille

Ⓞ

A SIGNET BOOK

NEW AMERICAN LIBRARY

TIMES MIRROR

PUBLISHER'S NOTE

This publication is designed to provide accurate and authoritative information in regard to the subject matter covered. It is published and put on sale with the understanding that the publisher is not engaged in rendering legal, accounting, financial, or other professional service. If expert assistance is required, the services of a professional should be sought.

To the memory of
Vivien Kellems

NAL BOOKS ARE AVAILABLE AT QUANTITY DISCOUNTS WHEN USED TO PROMOTE PRODUCTS OR SERVICES. FOR INFORMATION PLEASE WRITE TO PREMIUM MARKETING DIVISION, THE NEW AMERICAN LIBRARY, INC., 1633 BROADWAY, NEW YORK, NEW YORK 10019.

Copyright © 1982 by Jerome Tuccille

SIGNET TRADEMARK REG. U.S. PAT. OFF. AND FOREIGN COUNTRIES
REGISTERED TRADEMARK—MARCA REGISTRADA
HECHO EN CHICAGO, U.S.A.

SIGNET, SIGNET CLASSICS, MENTOR, PLUME, MERIDIAN AND NAL BOOKS are published by The New American Library, Inc., 1633 Broadway, New York, New York 10019

First Printing, May, 1982

1 2 3 4 5 6 7 8 9

PRINTED IN THE UNITED STATES OF AMERICA

Preface

In this country today, there is a black market amounting to an estimated $700 billion a year. This black market, or underground economy as it has been labeled, is larger than the official economies of most major nations. A combination of soaring inflation and outrageously high taxes has forced many Americans who are otherwise law-abiding citizens to hide much of their income from the IRS. By skimming cash from their businesses, moonlighting off-the-books, bartering for goods and services, and utilizing dozens of other techniques that we will look at in detail in the pages ahead, millions of middle-class Americans are able to cheat the IRS out of money they regard as rightfully theirs.

This book will offer you an inside look at this $700 billion underground economy and the people who participate actively in it. It will also introduce you to a number of tax rebels and would-be revolutionaries who have joined mail order churches, claimed Fifth Amendment protection on their tax returns, stopped filing altogether, and even attempted to establish a tax-free utopia in the South Pacific as a means of protesting against high taxes in the United States.

Finally, the last section of the book will show you how you can legally rearrange your own finances to reduce your personal tax burden and otherwise profit from the new American tax revolt.

Contents

Introduction

When the first man stood upright on this planet, his first order of business was to find enough food to keep himself and his family alive and to find shelter from the ravages of nature. Yet, no sooner had he accomplished this much in his daily struggle for survival when someone else would come along and try to take his meager possessions away.

It was bad enough having to share this hostile planet with one-celled protozoa, a curious assortment of lice and vermin, sharp-toothed denizens of the depths, flying reptiles, various cold-blooded amphibians, and a veritable rogue's gallery of hot-blooded mammals of different shapes and temperaments. Among this whole vicious collection, however, man's most formidable enemies turned out to be the other members of his own species. Yes, good old Homo sapiens has always harbored an avaricious streak unsurpassed by the scaliest reptiles and most ill-tempered mammals on planet Earth.

Man has always cast a lustful eye on the things that belong to his neighbor, and this inherent spirit of

1

larceny has not diminished noticeably. What has changed, though, is his modus operandi. In the old days, various tribes would simply cavort about the countryside, invade one another's territory, and have themselves a free-for-all until one group emerged victorious and walked off with all the valuables in sight.

In an effort to keep this sort of behavior from getting out of hand, our ancestors organized themselves into clans and larger social groupings for their collective defense. The strongest members of these various groups appointed themselves leaders, and they exacted tribute from the hoi polloi to help defray the cost of running the show. No one minded the system very much, as long as their self-appointed leaders were a bit more agreeable and a little less larcenous than their mutual enemies. Whenever a leader did happen to get carried away with his own power, as many leaders are apt to do, the rank-and-file would put up with it until the situation was no longer bearable, and then rise up and kick the rascal out of the clan, and possibly even lop off his head.

As the centuries rolled on and these social groupings grew larger and larger, many leaders developed the notion that they were divinely ordained to dictate to their fellow human beings. Some actually believed that they alone, among all the creatures on earth, were appointed by God to tell the other members of their clan how to run their lives. They passed restrictive laws against seemingly harmless behavior and forced the other members of their group to turn over most of the products of their labor so that they, the rulers, could live rich and comfortable lives without ever having to work.

This state of affairs existed for many centuries until the hoi polloi in various clans, now called countries, realized that as bad as their enemies in other countries were, their own rulers who were supposed to be protecting them were perhaps even worse. So, wherever the people were strong enough to get away with it, they launched revolutions to overthrow their dictators and create new systems that were more responsive to their own needs. These new systems went by different names: some called their country's system a democracy; others called it a republic; still others referred to it as a democratic republic, a social democracy, or variations on the same theme. But whatever name they went under, the new systems had one common characteristic: no longer could the leaders appoint themselves; from now on the hoi polloi would elect certain of their fellow citizens to represent them in a fashion that was beneficial to their collective needs.

This system, which remains with us today in the freer countries on planet Earth, has in varying degrees functioned relatively well over the past few hundred years. Human beings seem to be happier and more productive living in a free environment than under the restraints of a dictatorship. And, among all the countries of the world, it can safely be asserted that the United States of America made perhaps the most complete and democratic revolution in the history of the human race.

Yet, as far-reaching as the American Revolution was, and as good a system of government as it brought into existence, it has developed some serious problems over the decades. No system is perfect, and inequities are bound to emerge anywhere this side of paradise. Taxation, the means by which various governments obtain the money to pay for the services they provide, has never been popular with the people. At best, taxation is regarded as a necessary evil, along with sickness and death. Most people resent having a portion of their money taken away from them, even though they insist that the government that takes it away should provide a vast array of expensive services for them.

Under normal circumstances, the citizens of various countries pay their taxes grudgingly, holding back as much as they can reasonably get away with, in return for those services. But every now and then, in the course of human events, the cost of government services so glaringly outweighs the benefits derived from them that the citizenry rises up en masse and shouts its displeasure. The American Revolution itself was a revolt against outlandish taxes levied against the colonists by the king of England. On December 16, 1773, a group of colonists led by Paul Revere and Samuel Adams disguised themselves as Indians, boarded three ships in Boston Harbor, and tossed the cargo overboard to protest an unfair tax on tea. In retaliation, the English Parliment enacted five laws, referred to by American patriots as the Intolerable Acts, which limited the colonists' political and geographical freedom. The result of this was the First Continental Congress and, a short time later, an armed rebellion against the crown.

The revolution, however, was no guarantee that the American people would remain forever free of unjust and unpopular taxation. As the new nation grew in size and prosperity, the size and scope of the federal government, the several state governments, and the myriad local governments grew along with it. As government grew, its need for revenue also increased, and it searched for new and exotic methods of obtaining that revenue to fill its coffers. Government imposed tariffs and excise taxes on imports and exports, taxes on real estate and personal property, taxes on factories, industrial equipment, and so-called intangibles such as stocks, bonds, patents, and savings accounts. The states extended the tax structure to include every conceivable item of personal wealth. In New Hampshire, sheep were taxed at a rate of five shillings, swine at ten shillings, two-year-old steers at twenty-five shillings, and their three-year-old cousins at forty shillings. Massachusetts introduced the art of the tax rebate to bolster its ailing economy, offering reduced taxes to producers of hemp, flax, glass, and, perhaps most popular of all, to commercial beer brewers.

Throughout our history as a nation, there has been a recurring tendency to soften the tax blow for the wealthy who, after all, supply most of the loot to get politicians elected in the first place, and to sock the middle- and lower-income wage earners the hardest. The cry for "tax reform" to redress the inequities in our system of taxation has been with us right from the beginning. During the 1850s, several state governments amended their constitutions to include equal and uniform tax rates on all kinds of personal property. The intention was to reduce the tax burden on the average citizen and shift it a bit more heavily onto the backs of the wealthy property owners and industrialists. Intentions and results rarely coincide, however. Enforcement proved virtually impossible. In 1867, for example, taxes on such luxury items as pocket watches and clocks simply caused people to stop listing these trinkets among their items of wealth. By 1870, thousands of clocks and watches in Cook County, Illinois, had apparently ceased to exist. The same was true of horses, sewing machines, radios, and pianos once taxes were imposed on them. Suddenly, nobody owned them any more.

Government, you see, had started to create an *underground economy*. In their haste to avoid all these new taxes government was imposing, people searched for unique ways of hiding their wealth.

Certain items of wealth were not that easy to hide, however. You can't hide a railroad car or a factory in your broom closet the way you do your clocks and sewing machines when the tax man comes snooping around. But wealthy people did not get that way from lack of imagination, and certainly not from any shyness where the profit motive was concerned. As one philosopher put it, rich people are just like you and me, only more so. Therefore, wherever their taxable wealth was too bulky to be swept away in the broom closet or otherwise hidden from the revenue agent's view, the rich hired fancy lawyers to have valuations against their property lowered to a fraction of their true value, and then depreciated over time to help reduce their taxes even further. The age of the tax shelter had been ushered into existence so that the rich could remain that way while the hoi polloi paid through the nose for the privilege of living in a free society.

The most serious attempt to equalize the tax burden for all citizens came with the passage of the graduated income tax in 1913. Actually, an income tax had been enacted by Congress as early as 1864, then discontinued in 1872, and finally ruled unconstitutional in 1894 on grounds that it was not apportioned according to state population. Our representatives got around this by writing the Sixteenth Amendment which, in effect, legalized direct taxation of income. By graduating the income tax upward for higher levels of income, the measure was considered progressive; in theory, the wealthy were to pay a proportionately higher tax on income than the average earner.

But, again, intention and reality failed to find common ground. The tax code also provided for deductions and exclusions to be made against income so that an individual's taxable income could be reduced to a fraction of his total take for the year. By expert employment of the ubiquitous loopholes and shelters in the vast, impenetrable body of tax laws currently on the books, wealthy people have consistently been able to reduce their tax bite to a mere pittance and, in many cases, avoid paying taxes altogether. Indeed, some of those who have become most adroit at wriggling through the loopholes in the tax code are the politicians who created the tax laws in the first place. While he was campaigning for the presidency in 1980, it was revealed that Ronald Reagan had been paying virtually no taxes on a gross income of several million dollars a year. Corporate executives, rock stars, and other highly paid celebrities whose incomes range from six to eight figures a year likewise avoid paying any more taxes than the average-income wage slave whose taxes are withheld at the source.

Couple this with the monumental waste of taxpayers' dollars by the federal and local governments, the mismanagement of hundreds of millions of dollars worth of public funds, perks and fringe benefits for public employees that are not available for workers in the private sector (who foot the bill in the first place), corruption and graft on the part of high-ranking officials (much of which goes virtually unpunished), and you have the makings of a modern-day tax revolt. The problem has gotten so big and so complicated that Senator Russell Long of Louisiana, former chairman of the Senate Finance Committee, remarked after the passage of Proposition 13 in California, "The federal government is totally out of control. We do not know what we are doing here. We don't have any idea how much we're spending, how much we're taking in, how many agencies we have, how many programs we have. None of us know."

Senator Long was merely stating for the public record what millions of middle-class wage earners have known for years. Through a combination of escalating taxes on income and both real and personal property, and soaring inflation that pushes people into higher tax brackets and diminishes the buying power of their money, the real income of the average American wage earner dropped about 5 percent between 1970 and 1980. While the median income for all families with one wage earner working full time rose from $9,750 in 1970 to $19,950 in 1980, for a nominal increase of 105 percent, the amount taken by Social Security and federal income taxes during this same period increased 143 percent, from $1,338 to $3,251. This means that after-tax income went up 99 percent, from $8,412 in 1970 to $16,699 in 1980. When you factor in inflation for the period, however, real earnings in 1980 were only $7,976, a loss of $436 for the decade. Inflation for the decade averaged 7.7 percent a year, rendering the 1980 dollar less than half as valuable as the one earned in 1970.

In addition to the decimation of the people's wealth through taxes and inflation, American citizens have been forced to endure a humiliating tax on their time as well as their purses. In 1981, Americans spent 1.3 billion hours filling out over five thousand different types of government forms. This works out to an average of almost six hours for every man, woman, and child in the country. The agency responsible for more than half of this tax on the public's time and energy is—you guessed it—the Internal Revenue Service.

Tired of waiting for their elected representatives to make more than token reforms in the tax laws, the

American people have been taking matters into their own hands more volubly in the past few years. The underground economy of the last century, consisting of a handful of hidden clocks, pocket watches, pianos, and sewing machines, has grown today to an estimated $700 billion in unreported income and wealth. No less an authority than Sylvia Porter, whose figures coincide with those published in *The Wall Street Journal* and other reputable financial publications, claims that at least twenty million Americans fail to report all or a substantial part of their income to the IRS each year. In other words, the largest black market in the world exists not in the Soviet Union or some other dictatorship where private incentive is outlawed, but right here in the home of free enterprise, the United States of America.

Ironically enough, the federal government has gotten itself into a curious bind: the more people resist paying taxes, the more government is forced to raise taxes to make up the difference and attempt to balance the mounting budget deficit; the more government raises taxes, the more people hide their income and engage in underground or black market activities. We have what amounts to a Catch-22 situation, with no easy solutions in sight.

In the following pages we will take a look at the various methods, legal and illegal, that people use to reduce their tax exposure or avoid paying taxes altogether. We will meet a Rabelaisian cast of characters, including the self-styled queen of the underground economy and her army of nonfilers, the king of the Tax Rebellion, mail-order pastors and their new-found "religious" movements, leaders of legitimate tax-protest groups, ordinary citizens who barter their services and deal in cash, and many others, Then we will examine the various measures the IRS is planning (in some cases, already employing) in an effort to crack down on tax rebels. Finally, we will talk about what all this means to you and your money; what steps you can take now to minimize your personal tax burden legally; and what investment techniques you can utilize to increase your real wealth.

CHAPTER ONE

The Roots of Rebellion

Lucille Moran—The Queen of the Underground Economy

"It takes the mentality of a moron to try to dodge income taxes by the all-too-simple expedient of not filing a return at all. Only one out of every one hundred taxpayers who are liable to Federal income tax makes that attempt, but those 600,000 non-filers are a big headache to the Government."

Despite this sentiment, which was expressed by financial writer H. F. Millikin in 1963, there are enough nonfilers, morons or otherwise, in the country today for the IRS to have launched a major campaign against them. Paramount among the nonfilers is a fiery rebel named Lucille Moran, originally from Springfield, Massachusetts, who has made her home in the Florida Keys for the past ten years. Moran delights in being referred to as the queen of the underground economy, and she openly admits that she has not filed a tax return for more than fifteen years. Her first major confrontation with the IRS occurred in the early 1960s in Massachusetts, where she took on the combined wrath of the courts, lawyers, probate judges, and revenue agents in a battle over her father's estate. She decided then that she was being royally fleeced by the authorities, including her own lawyers, and she vowed never to pay taxes again.

Since then, Moran has made the study of the U.S. Constitution, the tax code, and the common law of the United States her full-time occupation. She created the Independent Bar Association of Massachusetts as a protest against the entrenched bench-bar establishment and appointed herself its president. She earns her living by representing other nonfilers throughout the country and by selling a package of booklets, pamphlets, and tapes instructing others how to get away without filing themselves. In a *Wall Street Journal* article dated March 20, 1980, reporter Jerry Landauer quoted an IRS memo that lamented, "Her clients have been traced to virtually every state in the country and Puerto Rico"; the article went on to describe Moran as "one of the most significant cases in the tax protest movement."

The literature that she offers for sale from her headquarters in Tavernier, Florida, includes how-to material with such exotic titles as *How to Refuse Income Taxes—Legally*; *Code of Ethics Subscribed to by Internal Revenue Employees*; *Taxation Depends on Confession—Pavlovian Style*; *Has There Been Jury Tampering?*; *Are Revenuers Covering up the Conspiracy against Veterans?*; *How Revenuers Are Violating Your First Amendment Rights by Practicing Church Law*; and many others that are equally provocative.

Although she refuses to reveal her age on the grounds that "a girl who tells her age will tell you anything," an educated guess would put her fairly close to seventy. Advancing age, however, has failed to diminish her passion about the tax protest movement, or the amount of time and energy she expends on its behalf.

"Tell me, Lucille," I asked her during a recent conversation, "how many tax rebels would you say there are in the country today?"

"Don't call me a rebel, baby," she replied, exhaling a puff of smoke from an ever present cigarette. (She rolled her own until a few years ago, but now smokes the packaged variety to save herself time. 'It's not the tobacco but all the gunk they put in it, the resins and flavor enhancers, that kills you, kiddo.') "I am a protester, a revolutionary in the tradition of Paine and Jefferson. The rebels are those idiots who file those Fifth Amendment returns, the ones where they fill in their name and address, and a statement that they refuse to answer any questions on the grounds that they might incriminate themselves. Those cretins are rebels."

"Whatever. How many nonfilers would you say there are in the country today?" I rephrased the question.

"Thirty or thirty-five million."

"Thirty-five million!"

"Well, maybe twenty-five million. Thirty-five's a bit high."

"Where do you get that figure from?"

"I've got my facts and figures, kiddo. I've got my sources."

Actually, determining exactly how many nonfilers there are in the country is virtually impossible. As an IRS special study team concluded in a twenty-nine-page report made available in 1980, "The consensus of the study group is that under current procedures and guidelines the service is unable to determine the scope of illegal tax protesters who are nonfilers and stop-filers." By the IRS's own admission, people who stop filing simply "disappear" from the computer system that existed through the end of 1980; people who change jobs and move periodically from one part of the country to another are especially hard to keep track of.

The Fifth Amendment protest movement, on the other hand, is easier to monitor, since those rebels voluntarily submit their names and addresses on their tax forms, along with their reservations about answering any questions. Again, according to IRS figures, there were 13,601 Fifth Amendment returns filed in 1979, twice the number filed in the previous year. This trend has IRS more than a little concerned. Financial columnist Sylvia Porter estimates that more than twenty million Americans are participating, to one extent or another, in the underground economy by failing to report all or a portion of their income to IRS each year.

Allowing for the fact that Lucille Moran's figure of twenty-five million nonfilers is considerably bloated, she and her army of followers are nevertheless large enough for IRS to have included her on its "enemies list" in 1972. (Amusingly enough, former New Mexico Senator Joseph Montoya's name also appeared on the list, directly above Moran's, a fact that caused no end of consternation among his colleagues in the Senate. Montoya and Moran were both identified as "possibly violent" by the IRS.)

Lucille Moran claims that, the IRS notwithstanding, she is not much inclined toward violence, but she admits to calling up IRS agents at home at 3 A.M. to "discuss my case" with them. She maintains that she is a night person who sleeps by day, and the early morning is "normal working hours" for her. She says all this tongue-in-cheek, understanding that her wee-hour phone calls are a trifle intimidating and unnerving, to say the least.

The special study conducted by the IRS states that IRS agents are growing increasingly concerned about their own safety. "IRS employees have experienced a wide range of threats, assaults and harassments from members of the illegal tax protest movement. In certain parts of the country—rural areas more than urban—violent protest has occurred. In many of these situations a seizure of property for nonpayment of taxes has evoked threats and assaults," the report reads.

Moran's early-morning phone calls to IRS agents are only the fun-and-game side of her raison d'être. She is dead serious about her philosophical and legal position as a tax protester. Her basic argument can be summed up as follows:

1. According to the IRS's own Code of Ethics, the income tax system of the United States is based on the voluntary compliance of American citizens. The word *voluntary*, Moran is fond of informing IRS agents in a never-ending barrage of correspondence and phone calls, does not mean "involuntary", and never has.

2. The income tax form is a violation of the *Miranda* decision, which requires public authorities to apprise citizens of their constitutional rights before asking them to divulge information that could be self-incriminatory. Moran maintains that for the tax form to be legal, these rights should be stated boldly on the top of the form.

3. The Internal Revenue Code is in violation of the Fourth and Fifth Amendments of the U.S. Constitution. The Fourth Amendment grants the right of the people to be "secure in their persons, houses, papers, and effects, against unreasonable searches and sei-

zures," while the Fifth states that no person "shall be compelled in any criminal case to be a witness against himself." According to Moran's argument, the IRS violates the Fourth Amendment by forcing people to turn over personal papers and records without due process, and it violates the Fifth by compelling people to report potentially damaging evidence against themselves.

This is the bare substance of her position, but it is only the starting point. From here she goes on to weave an intricate system of logic, accusing the IRS of practicing church law, of conducting an illegal Grand Inquisition, of making a mockery of the separation of church and state which is supposed to be the law of the land. She will quote you arcane points of natural law, common law, and other pertinent data regarding the legal traditions of the United States. Clearly, Lucille Moran does not fit H. F. Milliken's depiction of the nonfiler as having "the mentality of a moron." She is a highly intelligent, energetic, self-styled revolutionary—a protester who has done her homework and is well prepared in her continuing legal encounters with IRS. Despite her decade-and-a-half standing as a nonfiler, she has, by her own account, yet to spend a day in jail or pay a nickel in either fines or back taxes.

"How about those who follow you?" I asked her. "Have any of your clients been beaten by the IRS?"

"Oh, we've lost a few along the way. You can't win them all. For the most part, though, the ones who lose cave in when the opposition turns up the heat. It says something about the backbone of the modern American male. As soon as the going gets rough, he goes running off to a shyster—an entrenched bar lawyer—and that's the same thing as surrendering to the enemy. The IRS *wants* you to use a shyster. They know they've got you then. They all play by the same rules, you see. They put pressure on the shyster and he gets scared and cops a plea. You're playing by the enemy's rules when you hire a shyster."

"Yes, but doesn't the IRS have the deck stacked against you in the first place? Even if everything you say is true, they write the rules and the courts enforce them. What about IRS Code, Section 7203, which provides for a $10,000 fine and one year in jail for anyone who fails to keep records and file a return?"

"It's absolutely worthless. The only ones who get hit with that are those who file a return, put down phony information, and then sign their name to it. Then they get you for fraud. But since no criminal action can be taken against someone who refuses to make a voluntary confession in the first place, that section is unconstitutional, null and void, *ultra vires, ab initio,* of no effect, as if it had never been enacted."

"Don't they have the power to move in and seize your assets regardless of the finer points of law or constitutionality? They can get at your bank account, your . . ."

"I took everything out of my own name years ago. I closed down my checking account, and the house I live in is owned by the Church of the Celts, a church I established myself. So there's nothing to seize, kiddo."

"You're unique in that regard. Most people are more vulnerable than that."

"The fact is, the revenuers have been trying to toss me in the slammer for ten years now, and every time they come sniffing around I send them off with their tails between their legs. The problem with most people is that they're not versed in their rights. They rush to file an annual confession of their activities, as if it were their Easter duty, with a slavishness comparable to Pavlov's dogs. They act as though April 15 was their annual Holy Day of Obligation."

Indeed, the IRS *has* been trying to land her in "the slammer" for several years now, but so far she has proved an elusive target. Her most recent victory occurred in September 1980, when government attorneys dismissed charges against her for failing to file an income tax return.

In 1973, IRS special agents launched a full-scale criminal investigation against her, employing forty-seven agents from fifteen different states: Florida, Utah, Massachusetts, California, Arizona, Indiana, Idaho, Alaska, Louisiana, Georgia, Texas, West Virginia, Missouri, Kansas, and Washington. In April 1980, a Jacksonville, Florida, federal grand jury indicted her on two misdemeanor counts for failure to file returns for the years 1973 and 1974. Moran was jubilant when she learned that seven years of investigation and the expenditure of several hundred thousands of taxpayers' dollars failed to turn up an indictment on serious criminal charges.

She immediately filed a motion for a bill of particulars, charging that the IRS indictment against her was "too vague, misleading and unparticularized to permit defendant to adequately and properly prepare her defense." Moran was also able to demonstrate that she was being singled out for discriminatory treatment by the IRS since her name appeared on a special enemies' list prepared by the Internal Revenue's Political Intelligence Activities unit, which then deleted her name from the list in an effort to cover up the fact.

When the IRS failed to respond to her motion for a bill of particulars, Moran filed a new motion to dismiss her case because of the prosecutor's delay of trial. She cited Section 3161 (c) (1) of the Speedy Trial Act, which implements the Sixth Amendment right of every person to a speedy and public trial. U.S. attorneys, realizing that their case was weak, to say the least, dismissed charges against her "in the interest of justice."

Irwin Schiff—The King of the Tax Rebellion

The IRS, however, has been far more successful in its legal actions against the Fifth Amendment protesters—or rebels, as Lucille Moran dismisses them contemptuously. (Ironically enough, Moran's scorn for other tax protesters, particularly the Fifth Amendment variety, who fail to follow her "tried and true" techniques, matches the hostility she feels for her arch enemy, the IRS. According to her, the Fifth Amendment people have been "leading innocent people to the wolves" with their "incompetent" system of resistance.).

Most visible among the Fifth Amendment protesters is the self-styled king of the tax rebellion, a former investment counselor currently residing in Hamden, Connecticut, named Irwin Schiff. Schiff authored a book, *The Biggest Con: How the Government Is Fleecing You*, published in 1976, which spells out in detail his philosophy of government. According to Schiff, the United States government has perpetrated a giant hoax on the American public. The government destroyed our currency when it removed the dollar from the gold standard, the only true medium of exchange, and created the worthless scrip or fiat "unmoney" that is in circulation today. From this he concluded that since no one earns any "real money" today, no one is required to pay taxes.

Schiff describes taxation as "the arsenic in our system," and he claims that our country is "being poisoned by a tax system that (1) penalizes economic efficiency and destroys incentive while subsidizing inefficiency and encouraging unemployment, (2) diverts the nation's supply of capital to less efficient areas, (3) destroys jobs, (4) increases substantially the difficulty of the older workers to find employment, (5) promotes greater concentration of economic power, (6) compels those entering business to make Uncle Sam a 'silent partner' who puts up no capital yet demands more than half the profits, and (7) contributes directly to a lowering of public morality while increasing the influence of organized crime."

After writing his book, Schiff decided to become an active tax rebel. He read stories about men such as Arthur J. Porth and Jerome Daly, who were protesting against the income tax by filing returns with their names and addresses on them and the statement that they refused to answer any questions because of their rights under the Fifth Amendment. Daly and Porth had attracted a following by publicizing their position and conducting seminars in different parts of the country instructing others how to follow their example.

Schiff joined forces with Porth and Daly, and he proved to be even more successful at self-promotion than they were once he learned their techniques. He launched a national publicity tour, appearing on the leading radio and television talk shows, giving interviews to newspapers and magazines, openly advocating that people file Fifth Amendment protest returns. In effect, he was calling for a broad, middle-class revolution against the income tax in the United States.

Until this time, the IRS had been concerned enough about the activities of Porth and Daly and their following, limited in scope though they were. But when Schiff took the message to the networks and the major communications media, the IRS began to worry that the situation might get completely out of control. Here was a free, apparently sane American citizen going on the nation's airwaves and telling middle-class Americans not to pay their taxes. His radical approach was being delivered to virtually every household in the United States. Butchers, dentists, shoemakers, farmers, doctors, salesmen, entrepreneurs—the backbone of the American taxpaying public—were being encouraged to file Fifth Amendment protest returns by some bald, middle-aged man who was a guest on the "Phil Donahue Show." The citizenry was being whipped into a revolutionary frenzy, not by some long-haired, beaded relic of the "revolutionary" 1960s, but by an outwardly conventional American businessman.

The IRS could not take the chance that Schiff's argument might tap a responsive chord in the middle-class, American psyche. People were shocked enough about high taxes, inflation, and government waste without having a frenetic middle-aged radical working them into a fury. Former IRS director Donald Alexander admitted in the early 1970s that the one thing the United States government feared more than anything else was a wide-scale middle-class tax revolt. If everybody in the country decided to stop paying taxes tomorrow morning, he asked rhetorically, "What could we do about it? Throw the entire population behind bars?"

What the IRS decided to do about Schiff and the other Fifth Amendment protesters was to make examples of them and show the public the dire consequences of their actions. If the general public saw that these men could be penalized far beyond the tax dollars they owed the federal government, it would think twice before following their example. In the late

1970s the IRS launched a campaign to crack down on the Fifth Amendment protesters who were directing attention to themselves by the very nature of their protest. The IRS assigned a special team of agents to gather information and bring indictments against the leaders of the movement for willful failure to file income tax returns.

After a long-drawn-out court battle that ended in the summer of 1980, Irwin Schiff was found guilty of willful failure to file, and he was sentenced to six months in prison and a $10,000 fine. Through his attorney, Douglas Gilmore of Westport, Connecticut, he appealed his sentence. "The federal courts in this country are no better than Soviet courts," Schiff said to me in February 1981, while he was preparing his appeal.

"How's that?" I asked.

"The judge stacked the deck against me. He instructed the jury that my defense was not valid. Imagine that. He told the jury that I was not arguing in good faith and my defense was, therefore, invalid. My hearing was a farce."

"So where do you go from here?"

"I'm appealing, and I intend to bring this matter before the Senate Judiciary Committee. I'm going to tell the Congress and the American people that the income tax is invalid, not my arguments. Don't worry. I'm going to end the income tax in this country. It's only a question of when."

"How do you propose to do that?"

"By proving that the whole system is based on a fraud. The system is supposed to be voluntary, not compulsory. And how can we pay taxes on money we never earned in the first place since the government destroyed our money by taking us off the gold standard? IRS is discriminating against me because I'm the acknowledged leader of the tax rebellion. But I'm going to beat them in the end, don't worry."

"Do you still advocate filing a Fifth Amendment return?"

"I'm telling people not to file at all now. Just stop filing altogether."

"Oh?" I said, somewhat surprised. "You mean you've adopted Lucille Moran's approach?"

"I didn't adopt anybody's approach. I've just changed my own strategy. Moran is crazy. She accuses IRS of practicing church law and holding inquisitions. You don't need all that nonsense. All you need is the Constitution. IRS is violating our constitutional rights, it's as simple as that."

"How about Porth and Daly? Have they changed gears as well as you?"

"They're still telling people to file Fifth Amendment returns. I've developed a new approach and moved beyond them. Listen to me. I've got clients all over the country: Detroit, Boston, California, you name it. I sell my Freedom Kit telling people how to stop filing legally. I give lectures and seminars. I go on radio and television. I know more about taxes than anyone else in the country. You want to buy my kit? I'll sell you one. I'll sell you the transcript from my trial. People give me money just to fly out and talk to them. You think people would give me money if I was copying someone else? They want to learn my secrets, that's why. I'm the king of the tax rebellion. Everybody knows that now."

Lucille Moran, however, sees things a bit differently than Schiff does. When I informed her that he was now advocating the stop-filing approach, she laughed. "Those Fifth Amendment hucksters have been picking my brain for years, kiddo. I refuse to even talk to them anymore. All they're interested in is fame and fortune for themselves. They worship the almighty dollar. Now they found out their system doesn't work, so they've stolen mine. I wouldn't mind so much if they didn't lead innocent victims down the garden path with all that Fifth Amendment crap of theirs. All they're doing is stating grievances, you see. They never did learn the distinction between a grievance and a legal argument. I did all the homework, and now they're trying to cash in on it.

"I never went into this for the money, you know. I never went on the talk shows and solicited clients. People contacted me and I agreed to help them. But I've always told my people, don't go out of your way to attract attention to yourselves. Keep a low profile. Don't provoke IRS unnecessarily. Just drop out of the system and get your name off their computers. No, those other birds are only in it for the money. Me? I'm doing it because it's right. I'm just a tough old Yankee. I'm a revolutionary by birthright."

The Mail Order Ministers

An entirely different approach is taken by the Reverend Kirby J. Hensley, who founded the Universal Life Church in Modesto, California, during the early 1960s. By 1971 Hensley claimed to have ordained over a million people as ministers in his church, which has been referred to as "the fastest-growing 'religion' in the United States" in various newspapers and magazines. During a decade when the established churches were faced with a drop-out rate unprecedented in modern times, the smiling, bespectacled reverend from California somehow managed to convert nearly a million new people a year to his cause.

The mystery vanishes when we take a closer look at exactly what Hensley has been preaching. While he calls his organization a "religion," his message is more political than spiritual. According to the literature he publishes, "The Universal Life Church has no doctrine itself. It only believes in that which is right. . . . We recognize everyone's belief. . . . The purpose of the church is to bring freedom of religion to all people. We will ordain anyone without question of their faith, for life for a free-will offering."

The next paragraph spells out the true appeal of Hensley's church for millions of Americans throughout the country: "How does one establish a church under the UNIVERSAL LIFE CHURCH charter? The ULC will provide anyone with a charter if he or she wishes to open a church. The Headquarters of UNIVERSAL LIFE CHURCH will keep records of your church and file with the Federal Government and furnish you a *tax exempt status* [italics mine] and all you would have to do is to report your activities to Headquarters four times a year."

What Hensley has done, of course, is provide every individual in the country with a tax shelter under the guise of a religion simply for the asking—and the remission of a "free-will offering" which usually runs in the neighborhood of ten to twenty dollars.

The Reverend Kirby J. Hensley is the first to admit that he is as much concerned with political affairs as he is with religion. When he discusses politics, he unveils a philosophy of government that is three parts free-market anarchism and one part participatory democracy. "A lot of people today say," he wrote in one of his editorials, " 'you can't have absolute freedom, it'll destroy the country. It'll do this and that.' How do these people know that the country will go haywire if you don't have laws? Have they ever lived in a country where there is no law, but there was absolute freedom? I'm telling you that if you had absolute freedom tomorrow beginning at 7:00 in the morning, by the end of one year, you'd have less crime, less death, less sickness, less sorrow, less headaches than you have today. You'd see the country achieve greatness with people beginning to work for each other, because absolute freedom creates an atmosphere of life."

In 1970, Hensley attempted to launch another national political party called the Peoples Peace Prosperity Party. Its primary goal was to "organize independent thinking people into a strong third political party devoted solely to the task of returning government control to the people and re-establishing a true democratic form of government in the United States of America." Alas, it turned out that the tax-exempt umbrella Hensley was holding out to the American people, courtesy of his own church charter, was more enticing bait than the prospect of a new American grass-roots democracy under President Hensley. While his tax shelter-religious organization has continued to prosper over the years, his various political campaigns have never managed to get rolling.

The IRS has made several attempts to challenge the legal status of Hensley's Universal Life Church over the years, with varying degrees of success. In 1966, it challenged the tax-exempt status of Hensley's organization and won a judgment for $10,000 in back taxes. Hensley immediately filed an appeal and finally, on March 1, 1974 Federal Judge James F. Battin reversed the original decision and ordered the IRS to return the $10,000 plus interest and to award the Universal Life Church official status as a tax-exempt organization.

"How many church members do you have today?" I asked a New York City police officer who is Kirby Hensley's representative in the East.

"There are eleven million ordained ministers in the ULC today," he said, "and forty-five thousand chartered congregations throughout the country."

"You mean forty-five thousand separate churches in the ULC organization?"

"Any minister can apply to set up his own church under the ULC charter. Right now there are forty-five thousand of them, and we're growing every year. We built our own church building out here on Victory Boulevard on Staten Island, and we hold weekly services every Sunday which are open to the public. We were the first congregation in the country to do that."

"You're a New York City policeman, aren't you?"

"That's correct."

"Isn't that a bit odd, a policeman involved in a borderline operation like that?"

"Why? We have lots of police officers in the church, policemen, firemen, all kinds of public employees. Everything we do is perfectly legal. We're a legally recognized church under federal law. We hold regular services, keep records, just like we're supposed to."

"But isn't the real reason people join your church to avoid paying taxes?"

"We don't tell anybody what to do. We tell them, 'Look, once you become a member of our church you're entitled to all the benefits that go with it.' We didn't write the laws, the government did. We're just going along with them. Right now we're suing the IRS for $10 million."

"What for?"

"For discriminating against our religion and attempting to deprive us of our legal rights over the years. Now it's our turn to put them on the defensive."

"What happened to that group in upstate New York? Wasn't there an entire town that joined the ULC and put their houses in the church's name to avoid paying property taxes?"

"First they were off the tax rolls, then a state court ordered them back on, then they were off again after an appeal. Now the state's appealing that decision. That situation could go back and forth for years."

This police officer calls himself a bishop and conducts weekly Sunday services at his Staten Island church, as well as Thursday evening seminars instructing potential converts on how to set up their own church legally under the ULC charter and the tax benefits that go along with it. He publishes a church newsletter and disseminates other literature telling people that they can have "their own religious beliefs and receive the same tax benefits as other organized churches." During the tax season, ULC ministers and pastors can have their tax returns prepared for a fee by accountants affiliated with the Universal Life Church, and they can receive legal counseling by lawyers who also specialize in church-state law. All this is done openly.

In a later chapter we will take a look at the IRS's plans to try to put an end to it all.

The Search for the Tax-Free Utopia

Perhaps the most exotic tax rebels of all are those who want to create their own tax-free utopia outside the confines of the United States. For the past ten

years or so, this lusty band of rugged individuals has
been searching for an unclaimed island, for the purpose of homesteading it and creating a brand-new
country.

Now, you may think that in this day and age, with
the whole planet mapped and charted as it is, every
square inch of turf has already been claimed by
somebody or other. But this is not the case. In the
early 1970s, these hardy rebels managed to locate a
strip of unowned land somewhere between Tonga
and Fiji in the South Pacific. The reason the land was
still up for grabs was that no one could find it unless
he or she happened to be lost in the area during low
tide. At high tide the reefs were four feet under
water, and they constituted a treacherous hazard for
wayward mariners.

So, in January 1972, an Ohio oilman named Thur-
low Weed and a California lumberman named Robert
Marks sailed off to the South Pacific to stake their
claim. Weed and Marks planted the flag of the newly
created Republic of Minerva (a gold torch in a gold
circle against a blue background) and sent a declaration of sovereignty to over a hundred countries.
Well financed by other American industrialists, these
gentlemen hoped to develop the reefs at a cost of
$15,000 an acre, then subdivide the island and sell
shares to other tax rebels who were interested in moving to their tax-free paradise.

We will never know whether the plan could have
been carried to fruition, for the entire project was
sabotaged by the only political ruler on earth who
took notice of the fledgling new Republic. His Im-
perial Majesty, Haufa' ahou Tupou IV, the king of
near-lying Tonga, was furious when he heard what
was going on only two hundred miles away from his
royal domain. After handpicking some of the most

bloodthirsty convicts from the Tongan jails, the king outfitted his yacht with a few howitzers and led his merry pack on a mission to occupy the new country. By June 1972, the dream was all over for the intrepid tax rebels; it was aborted by a latter-day king who did not share their lofty notions of individual liberty.

(The question arises: if you can't defend Utopia against the king of Tonga, what do you do when Gautemala attacks?)

Down but not completely defeated, the Minervans jettisoned the idea of homesteading an unowned island and began to entertain the possibility of starting a revolution on one that was already under rule. Overturning the United States government sounded a bit ambitious, particularly after the run-in with Tonga, so the rebels searched for another tropical paradise where the natives were being treated like second-class citizens.

Finding an island where the citizenry was oppressed and damned unhappy about it was as easy as finding thumbtacks in your bathwater. The process of selection narrowed down to those areas where the conditions for revolution seemed especially ripe. Finally, they located their spot.

The island of Abaco was under the dominion of the Bahamian government, and there was considerable agitation for independence among the islanders, who were being treated rather rudely by the Pindling regime in Nassau. Beginning in 1973, a group of American tax rebels, led by Mike Oliver, a disgruntled Lithuanian refugee who was the architect of the Minerva project, moved to Abaco and established the Abaco Independence Movement.

Oliver set out immediately to educate the natives about the virtues of the American Revolution, particularly as defined in the writings of Jefferson, Paine, and other individualistic patriots. When the revolution came to Abaco, Oliver wanted it to be the right kind of revolution—no Marxist dictatorship à la Fidel Castro, if you please. Toward this end, Oliver sponsored a series of lecture tours featuring American economists whose philosophy of government coincided with his own. One of his first guests was John Hospers, a California philospher and disciple of Ayn Rand, who was immediately branded a "subversive" by the Pindling government, which banned his book, *Libertarianism*, from the island and declared Hospers persona non grata on Bahamian soil.

Mike Oliver's main goal was for the island to secede and be restyled as a laissez-faire society under a constitution that spelled out what the new government *would not* be permitted to do. It would not issue money, restrict trade in any way, establish a school or church, own property or business, establish mandatory welfare programs, grant franchises, subsidize business, initiate wage and price controls, or engage in a host of other activities. It *would* keep the peace via a court and judicial system, defend the islanders from attack (by the king of Tonga presumably), guarantee copyrights and patents, and protect the health, life, and property of the people.

The major problem with Oliver's movement was that, while Abaco was a grand place to spend a vacation, it was questionable exactly how many people would actually be inspired to pack up and live there. The island had sun, sand, and sea aplenty, but little else to offer the crusading individualist desirous of a reasonably civilized lifestyle. It was almost entirely undeveloped, and the cost of living was excessively high, since virtually everything had to be imported. Oliver hoped to overcome these hurdles by establishing a free trade zone without taxes of any kind, thereby attracting industry and people to the island. Theoretically, a lot of corporations would find the climate congenial for business, and they would be enticed to improve the island and create jobs.

Other intangible obstacles remained, however. If the islanders succeeded in gaining their independence, were they likely to allow their revolution to be shaped by white capitalist intruders from "imperialist" America? Or would they open the prisons and tell the convicts to toss the white folk into the sea? What guarantee did anyone have that Oliver could control events, like a capitalistic Lenin, once the revolution got going?

In the end, it was not the Pindling regime in Nassau or native rambunctiousness that put an end to Oliver's Abaco Independence Movement. Internal bickering, disagreements among various factions, and political infighting brought the effort to a standstill. Oliver's purist, tax-free, capitalist utopia degenerated into a ragtag reform movement for home rule and local control. Oliver and his people gradually lost interest, and the organization self-destructed in 1977.

Once again, Mike Oliver focused his attention on the South Pacific. This time he zeroed in on the New Hebrides, an archipelago northwest of Fiji, beyond the reaches of Tonga's gunboat.

As early as 1971, an associate of Oliver had bought a large spread of land on Gaua, one of the Banks Islands on the northern end of the archipelago. The New Hebrides already had a reputation as a tax haven, but when the British-French condominium government that ruled the islands passed new laws restricting landownership and development by foreigners, Oliver lost interest in the site as a possible home for his new country.

Early in 1975, Robert Poole, a journalist and editor of the libertarian magazine *Reason*, reported after a month-long trip to the New Hebrides that conditions were ripe for an independence movement on the Banks and Torres islands at the northern extremity of the archipelago. Poole advised Oliver to contact the leader of the Na-Griamel movement on Espiritu Santo Island, Jimmy Stevens, who was interested in establishing a breakaway government congenial to Oliver's interests. Oliver, who was already growing disenchanted with his Abaco Independence Movement, sent one of his aides to meet with Stevens in June 1975. The meeting went well and on June 3, 1975, Oliver created the Phoenix Foundation, which was to be a capitalistic Peace Corps of sorts, dispensing economic and political advice to the various independence movements on the islands. Among the board members of the Phoenix Foundation were best-selling author and psychologist Nathanial Branden, who was also a former associate of Ayn Rand; philosopher John Hospers of Abaco fame; financial writer and gold bug Harry Schultz; retired Air Force officer Hank Phillips; Mike Oliver; and Robert Poole.

Jimmy Steven's Na-Griamel movement had been involved in a conflict of its own with the National party (later known as the Vanuaaku party), which was headquartered in Vila, the British-French administrative center on the southern island of Efate. The National party, primarily under British influence, had grown increasingly socialistic, calling for the confiscation of all undeveloped European land without compensation. On this issue, the British and French were themselves in conflict; the French had substantial economic interests in the area, namely nickel and tin deposits in New Caledonia, five hundred miles to the south, and a booming tourist trade in Tahiti. The British, with no such interests, were allowing Marxist elements to dominate the National party, a development that meant potential trouble for the French.

Na-Griamel, on the other hand, was openly capitalistic and anti-Marxist. Its symbol was a black hand shaking a white hand below some native leaves that traditionally stood for racial harmony. Na-Griamel, under the leadership of Jimmy Stevens, a burly black man with a bushy white beard, advocated an open-door policy for all foreigners who wanted to help develop the island. Stevens recognized France as his natural ally in his battle against the National party, and in July 1975 he led a Na-Griamel delegation to Paris for the Bastille Day celebrations, at the invitation of President Giscard D'Estaing. In August 1975, following the first elections ever held in the New Hebrides, Na-Griamel won fifteen of sixteen seats on Espititu Santo, while allies of the movement won two-thirds of the seats in Vila, the home base of the condominium government. However, when national elections were held three months later, the National party came out a solid winner over Na-Griamel and its allies. Jimmy Stevens immediately charged the opposition with election fraud, and he wrote a letter to Mike Oliver requesting his assistance.

Stevens demanded new elections, and he threatened to lead a secessionist movement in the northern islands. He signed a contract with Oliver, granting Oliver the right to produce and market gold and silver coins bearing the slogan "Individual Rights for All" beneath Stevens's own likeness. Together with Oliver, Na-Griamel proclaimed the last day of 1975 as Independence Day for a group of northern islands, and honorary citizenship in the new Na-Griamel Federation was offered to all who made a substantial contribution to the new country.

And then, as the saying goes, things got interesting.

Oliver wanted more than a promise from the flamboyant Jimmy Stevens that the new nation would be a tax-free, laissez-faire paradise. Jimmy Stevens seemed like a nice enough chap, charismatic to the extreme with his billowing white beard, colorful robes swaddling his girth, and harem of innumerable women of all ages, but Oliver wanted to be sure that Stevens was committed to the same principles he was and not merely using Oliver to establish a tropical kingdom for himself.

Together with a group of doctors and dentists who were interested in starting a clinic in the new country, and a radio technician who wanted broadcasting rights, Oliver left for Espiritu Santo to meet with Stevens and other Na-Griamel leaders. Oliver also dispatched Robert Poole and David Sutton, an ex-Marine who was an expert at jungle survival and military tactics, to teach the islanders combat techniques and to train them ideologically.

While Poole and Sutton were giving instruction in hand-to-hand combat techniques as well as the benefits of a tax-free, laissez-faire paradise, Oliver's radio technician set up a broadcasting station in the village of Tanafo, a Na-Griamel stronghold. The programing was simple and direct; it featured news reports on what was happening in the outside world, alternating with Jimmy Stevens's taped speeches to his people. Oliver, meanwhile, occupied his time coauthoring, with David Sutton, a constitution for the new country. He was determined to play the role of a latter-day Thomas Jefferson in every respect.

The constitution they finally drafted is an intriguing attempt to spell out the individual rights guaranteed in the U.S. Bill of Rights (and then some), utilizing the bastardized New Hebridean language, which is a kind of English-french pidgin known as "bichlemar." The first amendment, which reads, "*Evri man mo evri woman emi gat rit to lif blo im. Evri man, sepos i swet, i gat rit kip wat i ern*," can roughly be translated as, "Every man and every woman always has the right to the life which belongs to him. Every man, suppose I sweat, I got the right to keep what I earn." The third amendment guarantees the right to bear arms: "*Evri man, mo evri woman, i gat rit own musket. I gat rit own eni kin musket.*" ("Every man and every woman has the right to own a musket, any kind of musket). The twenty-first amendment prohibits government censorship: "*Kapman i gat no power lo ae wat buk i se, mo wat cinema i se, mo wat magazin i se*" ("Government officials have no power to say what books I read, or what movies I see, or what magazines I read"). All in all, there were twenty-four separate amendments detailing individual rights under the law.

This much accomplished, Jimmy Stevens issued his Declaration of Independence for Na-Griamel on December 27, 1975, and he ordered the condominium government to leave the northern federation of islands by April 1 of the following year. On December 28, Radio Tenafo announced that the new country of Na-Griamel had "evicted the British and French as colonialists, not as residents. . . . The new government will levy no taxes, regulate no one's life. Instead, it will serve to carry on minimal functions."

On December 30, a blustery Tuesday in New York, Na-Griamel leaders James Garae Bakeo, Timothy Weles Nafakon, and Osea Gavidi presented their credentials to the United Nations and deposited copies of their declaration of sovereignty. They were ignored, however, at the insistence of the British-French condominium government, which maintained that the revolutionaries did not have the backing of the people.

As the April 1 deadline for the condominium government to vacate the northern islands approached, Jimmy Stevens grew more and more belligerent. Against Mike Oliver's wishes, he announced over Radio Tenafo that he would stampede thousands of heads of cattle against government offices if they failed to leave, and he promised to launch a campaign of "fire and blood."

Mike Oliver was outraged. Here he was trying to portray himself as a latter-day Jefferson, a man of enlightenment and reason, and his polygamous ally was turning into a Polynesian firebrand, threatening to stampede the island with a herd of cattle. Oliver told Stevens not to alienate the French, whom he regarded as their natural ally in the struggle, and he had his philosopher friend, John Hospers, write a letter to France apologizing for Jimmy's rather intemperate behavior.

The letter worked. Once again, Jimmy Stevens was invited to Paris by President Giscard D'Estaing who, apparently, was inclined to make allowances for his quaint excesses of speech. Before he left, Jimmy Stevens was instructed in no uncertain terms to cool his inflammatory rhetoric about fire and blood. The French were willing to help, if only to protect their own economic interests in the area, but the patrician French president was not about to lend even tacit support to some tropical terrorist.

Jimmy Stevens put on a suit and tie for the occasion and left his colorful regalia and harem at home. Giscard D'Estaing was mollified, and he helped draft a moderate plan calling for elections in November 1977, then again in 1979, toward final independence by July 30, 1980. The elections would be for representatives in the new National Assembly, filled exclusively by New Hebrideans, which would govern the new country when it was declared an independent nation.

In the first of these two elections, the National party, now going under the name Vanuaaku, lost considerable ground to Na-Griamel and its more moderate ally, the Natatok party. The leader of Vanuaaku, Father Walter Lini, who was supported by the World Council of Churches and the United States Department of State, refused to honor the election results. Lini declared the election null and void, and issued his own Declaration of Independence under the People's Provisional Government for all of the New Hebrides. In effect, there were now two governments ruling the islands: Lini and his socialistic People's Provisional Government, which refused to vacate the premises, and the National Assembly, under the leadership of the Na-Griamel and Natatok parties. The British-French condominium administration, which was supposed to monitor the results of the election, was itself powerless to act; the British tacitly supported the Lini government by looking the other way, while the French backed the National Assembly, which, after all, was their own creation.

What to do?

Tension mounted as the two opposing governments issued contradictory proclamations. Lini established his own police force, addressed his aides as "commissar," levied high taxes on merchants and businessmen which were collected by his policemen, and issued passes for $1.00 apiece for anyone who wanted to travel from one island to another. Na-Griamel raised its own flag over Tenafo, built an airstrip with the help of French engineers, and announced the beginning of airline service on Air-Melanesia. While all this was going on, Mike Oliver and his Phoenix Foundation began to see events slip further and further beyond their control.

In March 1979, with the political and economic life of the New Hebrides in shambles, Jimmy Stevens took it upon himself to journey to the United States to attempt to round up support. As Oliver had predicted, however, his pleas fell on deaf ears. During the following months, the situation on the islands continued to deteriorate. Acts of physical violence between the warring factions grew increasingly common. Elections were held again in June 1979, with results similar to the preceding election. Once again Father Lini ignored the returns and proclaimed himself prime minister of the People's Provisional Government, and he backed his statement up with the power of his police force. The impasse continued.

In March 1980, Jimmy Stevens journeyed to France with nine of his allies, and they complained that they were being subjected to violent attacks by the Lini government. One delegate claimed that his house had been burned down by Lini's policemen, others that they were beaten up and threatened. President Giscard D'Estaing appointed a French lawyer, Armand Lizop, and an associate of Oliver, F. Thomas Eck, a lawyer from Nevada, as advisers in the situation. The two lawyers were commissioned to devise a new plan whereby the islands would be divided into a confederation of four districts, each of which would be permitted to draft its own constitution and be more or less self-governing.

On April 9, 1980, twenty chiefs representing every island in the New Hebrides assembled for a convention to vote on the French proposal. For eight days the chiefs negotiated, compromised, and, on April 17, finally settled on a new constitution for the federation. All chiefs, including a representative of Lini's government, signed the document. Lini, who was opposed to any diminution of his own power, could hardly be the sole dissident in such a public display of unanimity.

When the convention was over, however, and the various chiefs returned to their own villages, Father Lini acted to keep the plan from being implemented. He invited the American ambassador to Fiji to accompany him on a tour of the southern islands and informed him that subversives were bent on overthrowing his democratically elected government. On the island of Tanna, near the southern tip of the archipelago, the ambassador told the natives in a public speech that the United States firmly supported Father Lini's government and would not tolerate any attempts to change the status quo. The Tannese, whose chief had recently returned from the convention where he had voted to support the new federation, were inflamed by the speech and seized the Vanuaaku government office on the island. A few days later, on May 27, the British sent in troops to retake the building.

Meanwhile, on the northern end of the archipelago, Jimmy Stevens decided that direct confrontation was his only hope after all. On the morning of May 28, he led a march on the government office in Espiritu Santo and succeeded in occupying the premises. Immediately, Radio Tenafo proclaimed that the new federation of Vemarana was officially in existence. The British-French condominium government and its puppet regime, the Vanuaaku party, no longer had any authority on the islands, Stevens said.

Once again, the opposing factions were deadlocked. Lini's police force, with the help of British troops, controlled the southern half of the archipelago, while Na-Griamel and its allies openly flew the flag of the federation of Vemarana on the northern islands. The battle lines were drawn, with each side refusing to back down. "All law and order have broken down," Father Lini wired the British government as gunfire ruled the streets of the once-peaceful archipelago.

Growing more and more alarmed that they had the makings of a full-scale revolution on their hands, the French flew in fifty-five riot police from nearby New Caledonia, and the British landed two hundred marines on Efate, the headquarters of the condominium government. The United States Department of State, for its part, announced that it was investigating the activities of American citizens who "may have interfered in the internal affairs of the New Hebrides." Specifically, the State Department sent investigators, along with special agents from Interpol, to Carson City to look into the Phoenix Foundation and a gold- and silver-trading firm owned by Mike Oliver. The investigators were instructed to determine if Oliver and his associates had violated the Logan Act, which prohibits American citizens from interfering in the affairs of foreign countries.

"If they want to use the Logan Act," said Mike Oliver indignantly, "let them use it on the National Council of Churches, which supports the World Council of Churches in full knowledge that some of the money is used to buy weapons for terrorists."

"How did it all turn out?" I asked Robert Poole in February 1981.

"In the end it was Australia which played the key role in crushing Na-Griamel," said Poole.

"Australia? How did they get involved?"

"The British and French were themselves in conflict. So Lini asked the government of Papua New Guinea for military aid. Well, Australia runs New Guinea, which is strategically important to them, and they sent in troops, planes, and patrol boats. The British and French stood by while Australia moved in and crushed the federation."

"I guess it was an easy way out for England and France."

"I suppose so."

"What happened to Jimmy Stevens?"

"He's in jail now, currently serving a thirteen-year sentence. The government also kicked out several hundred French citizens who were sympathetic to Na-Griamel, as well as Mike Oliver and the rest of Phoenix."

"So you're all persona non grata down there now?"

"Yes."

"What's next? Where do you go from here?"

"Why don't you ask Mike Oliver about it? I'm sure he's got something else in the works."

Yes, the roots of rebellion continue to run wide and deep. The nonfilers and stop-filers, the Fifth Amendment protesters, the mail order ministers, the new-country advocates in search of a tax-free utopia, and other antitax rebels who openly operate on the far side of the law are, if anything, stepping up their various activities in opposition to the tax system of the United States of America. Irwin Schiff began serving his six-month sentence for failing to file a tax return on February 18, 1981; Mike Oliver is accused of violating the Logan Act; Lucille Moran is continually hounded by IRS agents who, by her own account, are trying to land her in "the slammer"; yet the underground economy continues to grow in size and scope, and the rebellion continues.

"The federal income tax will soon be over as increasing numbers of Americans refuse to voluntarily assess themselves," Schiff told reporters as he was led off to jail. The IRS has joined the battle with greater vigor than ever before and is adopting countermeasures to crack down on the radicals. By its own admission, the IRS is now using the "vinegar" approach more and more frequently, after having learned that its "honey" measures don't work.

Let's take a look now at some orthodox tax rebels who choose to do battle within the confines of the law. In recent years, a good deal of antitax sentiment has risen to the surface of American life and been channeled into more acceptable, legal methods of protest. Tax resistance has become a "respectable" middle-class activity and, because of this respectability, millions of Americans who regard themselves as patriotic, law-abiding citizens have decided to join the battle.

CHAPTER TWO

The Rebellion Surfaces

Taxpayers Unite—The National Taxpayers Union

While most Americans would never dream of joining the ranks of the tax radicals and self-styled revolutionaries, their sense of outrage against a less than equitable taxing system is no less real.

During the past few years, a number of tax-protest organizations advocating legal resistance to high taxes have come into existence. Perhaps the most visible among them is the National Taxpayers Union (NTU), headquartered in Washington, D.C., under the chairmanship of a young, free-spirited individualist named James Dale Davidson. Davidson, an articulate and well-educated lobbyist with the looks of a film star, is the author of a recent best-seller called *The Squeeze*.

In his book, Davidson made the point that more and more middle-class Americans are forced to participate in the underground economy because they are being "squeezed" financially by the federal government. First there is the money squeeze, which cheapens the value of the dollar with government-created inflation; then there is the tax squeeze, which pushes wage earners into higher tax brackets without indexing these brackets for inflation. Third, according to Davidson, there is the quality squeeze, which he views as a form of indirect inflation; instead of raising prices, manufacturers lower the quality of their products, which amounts essentially to the same thing. Next there is the health-care squeeze, whereby people receive indifferent, less-personalized medical treatment at ever rising prices; fifth, there is the housing squeeze, with the average American paying astronomical prices for houses constructed with shoddier material and less reliable labor than were available a few decades ago; sixth, there is the legal squeeze, which requires people to hire lawyers for nearly every routine transaction they make (buying and selling homes, getting a divorce, going into business, and so forth). And, finally, there is the bureaucratic squeeze resulting from the enormous amount of paperwork involved in complying with government rules and regulations.

Davidson struck a responsive chord with his book, since the type of "squeezes" he is talking about affect all of us where it hurts the most: in the pocketbook. The National Taxpayers Union is a privately funded organization with a network of local taxpayer groups scattered across the country. While it is not affiliated with any particular political party, its message is distinctly conservative, with a libertarian twist. The NTU newsletter, aptly titled *Dollars and Sense*, is full of quotes from politicians who have a record of combating government waste and high taxation, such as William Proxmire, William Roth, Jack Kemp, and William Byrd, and former Governors Dolph Briscoe of Texas and the late James Longley of Maine. The union's board of advisors boasts such disparate names as actress Elizabeth Ashley, economists Henry Hazlitt and William Simon, and writers Harry Schultz and Robert Sherrill (the latter built his reputation on the left side of the political spectrum).

According to literature disseminated by the NTU, the federal debt amounts to some $10 trillion, or nearly $120,000 for every man, woman, and child living in the United States. Davidson claims that these figures are compiled from official Treasury Department figures, and they include interest on the public debt, loan and credit guarantees, insurance commitments, international obligations, and other debts incurred by the federal government.

"While you've been working to make ends meet," Davidson says in a fund-raising appeal, "politicians have been racking up debts—which you'll have to pay."

Other studies by Davidson indicate that "$3 billion is stolen annually from health programs," the U.S. government has funded over $250 billion for foreign aid, including . . . money for the U.S. to finance both sides in 14 wars during the last 20 years, billions are wasted annually on . . . totally ineligible welfare recipients, $200 million is spent annually to . . . shower favored professors with grants," so that "there are 23 biographies of Isaac Newton in the Library of Congress." Davidson maintains that the interest on the national debt is now $90,000 a minute.

In an effort to fight all this waste, which results directly in rising inflation and higher taxes, the National Taxpayers Union is currently working for the passage of two constitutional amendments. The first would limit the federal income tax to a maximum of 25 percent, a sharp drop from its present ceiling of 50 percent. The second is a balance-the-budget amendment that would prohibit the government from ever spending more than it takes in. Davidson says that the approval of thirty-four states is required to force Congress to enact this amendment into law, and so far over thirty states have adopted it. The honorary cochairmen of his balance-the-budget committee are William Simon and Dolph Briscoe, who is now a congressman. Davidson states that more than 180 members of Congress support his efforts.

Besides working for the enactment of these amendments to the U.S. Constitution, the NTU actively lobbies in Congress for lower taxes and reduced spending and helps local groups organize taxpayers unions of their own. After getting off to a slow start from its inception in 1969, the National Taxpayers Union has grown to a paid membership of approximately one hundred thousand. Davidson says that NTU membership doubled in 1978 alone, right after the passage of Proposition 13 in California.

"The American Revolution was really the work of about twenty people," Davidson remarked optimistically during a recent interview. "When you have high taxes, it is very hard for new enterprise to compete. High taxes reward monopoly privilege. High taxes prevent people from changing their pattern of discretionary income. Institutional egoism gets substituted for personal egoism. The liberal ideal was really defeated in this century."

When Davidson talks about liberalism, he is referring to the classical liberalism of Adam Smith and Jeremy Bentham. While classical liberalism is close to contemporary American conservatism philosophically, Davidson prefers the label *libertarian* when describing himself. The low-tax, anti-big government message is considered conservative by most people today, but Davidson sees contradictions in conservative thinking.

"Conservatives lack compassion. They're also guilty of gross oversights, like their failure to criticize the Pentagon."

Davidson has better things to say about Howard Jarvis, the so-called Father of Proposition 13 in California, which was supported by the National Taxpayers Union. He regards Jarvis as an authentic hero, a rugged individualist in the grand old American tradition.

"The problem with Jarvis is that he really isn't a movement at all," said Davidson. "He doesn't tie into any network. Jarvis is a one-man band. If he fell under a truck tomorrow, his movement would be over."

Howard Jarvis—The Father of Proposition 13

The passage of Proposition 13 on June 6, 1978, was, perhaps, the most dramatic and symbolic event to date in the American antitax movement.

Howard Jarvis, a wealthy real estate speculator and entrepreneur who emigrated from Utah to California in 1931, had been dabbling on the fringes of Republican party politics most of his life. After selling his home-appliance business in 1962 for a substantial profit, Jarvis retired and devoted himself full time to the struggle against a major grievance of his: soaring property taxes in California.

His early efforts to organize a grass-roots tax protest movement were not especially notable. His United Organization of Taxpayers never did sign up more than a few hundred members in the mid-1960s, and these were described as "a bunch of losers" by others who were sympathetic to his cause. In 1968 Jarvis and Philip Watson, the property assessor for Los Angeles County, were unsuccessful in an effort to get a tax limitation initiative on the ballot. In 1970 Jarvis lost an election for a seat on the State Board of Equalization when his opponent succeeded in portraying him as something of a screwball. The same year, then again in 1972, he failed to qualify a tax limitation initiative for the ballot because of a lack of signatures.

Daunted, but not yet ready to accept defeat, Howard Jarvis continued in his effort to build a broad-based tax-resistance organization and to get his initiative on the ballot. Finally, in 1977, as public sentiment against rising taxes increased throughout the state, Jarvis was introduced to Paul Gann, a more orthodox conservative who was the leader of the People's Advocate, an antitax group based in Sacramento. Gann's organization had already collected three hundred thousand signatures to get an initiative on the ballot in 1978, while Jarvis had four hundred thousand signatures of his own; five hundred thousand were needed to qualify.

Despite their common crusade, neither Gann nor Jarvis had much use for each other. Gann openly referred to Jarvis as a clown and a buffoon, while Jarvis felt patronized by Gann's patrician manner. Allies of both men prevailed, however, and were able to overcome their personal animosities. It was simply a matter of arithmetic; together they had the signatures, individually they would fail again.

It has often been said that politics makes strange bedfellows, and this truism was never more apt than in the political marriage of Howard Jarvis and Paul Gann. After the passage of Proposition 13, Jarvis would be remembered as the architect of the bill.

Indeed, he openly campaigned for the role, appearing on radio and television, giving hundreds of speeches throughout the country, buttonholing scores of congressmen and senators in Washington, D.C., and brazenly warning them to get in line or else risk losing their jobs, and writing an autobiograpy entitled, *I'm Mad As Hell*, whose title he borrowed from the berserk television anchorman played by Peter Finch in *Network*. Yes, later on Howard Jarvis effectively minimized Paul Gann's role in the passage of Proposition 13, but there is no question that in May 1977 they came together out of common need. After more than a decade of individual failure, they could finally make success theirs by joining forces.

The climate had never been better for the passage of a tax limitation initiative in California than it was in 1978. In 1950 there was one state employee for every thirty residents in the state. A decade later the ratio had narrowed to 1:25, and by 1978 it stood at 1:15. In the ten-year period stretching from 1968 to 1978, the budget had tripled from $5 billion to $15 billion. The tax rate in the state increased at a pace nearly three times that of personal income. While the population of Los Angeles declined 2 percent between 1968 and 1978, city expenditures increased almost 169 percent. Assessments on real estate and personal property in California increased 15 percent in one year alone, from 1977 to 1978, resulting in an additional $10 billion in property taxes. State employees received a total compensation package, including salaries, paid vacations and holidays, and pensions, that was 25 percent higher than workers in private industry whose taxes paid for it all. All in all, residents of the state were more than fed up with it, and years of campaigning by Jarvis were finally paying off. At the age of seventy-five, after having retired from business sixteen years earlier, Howard Jarvis found his constituency as a political messiah. He was the right man at the right time with the right message. His time had come.

"If I'm a nut, I'm in pretty good company," Jarvis remarked when the struggle to get Proposition 13 enacted into law was over. "A million and a half Californians, including Ronald Reagan, signed our petitions. Milton Friedman, Neil Jacoby, and Arthur Laffer supported 13. And Friedman even taped some TV commercials for us at no charge."

Jarvis denied that Proposition 13 was strictly a middle-class tax revolt, as *Time* magazine had characterized it.

"This was across the board. We got 40 percent of the minority and lower-income vote. We got about 60 percent of the vote of the middle class. We got practically all of the vote of the wealthy. When you roll up a 65 percent vote in a state the size of California, there's no way to say that this was an action of any particular class."

This evaluation is supported by Robert Kuttner, the author of *The Revolt of the Haves*, who is an avowed liberal and certainly no fan of tax-revolt legislation.

"Proposition 13 was the result of shifting taxes, unresponsive politicians, and unusually opportune timing," Kuttner wrote in his book. "So effectively did Jarvis mobilize general economic discontent into an income transfer for the rich, that even the poor voted, by a slight majority, for Proposition 13.

"Though the tax cuts heavily favored upper-income groups, people with incomes over $25,000 actually voted for Proposition 13 by slightly less than the state average: upper-income voters approved, 61 to 39. The middle class, hard hit by inflation and rising state income taxes, voted yes almost exactly 2 to 1. . . . The poor, with incomes below $8,000, most of whom rent, supported Proposition 13 by 55 to 45."

Jarvis and Kuttner interpreted the election results differently, however. Jarvis viewed them as a ringing, across-the-board endorsement of his tax limitation campaign, while Kuttner maintained that Jarvis skillfully sold his proposal to those who could not benefit from it.

In essence, Proposition 13 limited property taxes to 1 percent of fair market value. It also stipulated that no new taxes could be imposed by state or local government without the approval of two-thirds of the voters. Property assessments were frozen at 1975-76 levels, allowing for 2 percent annual increases for inflation. In actual dollars, a homeowner with a house carrying a fair market value of $150,000 (a mere pittance in a state where housing values have leaped astronomically) could not be taxed more than $1,500 a year, or one percent of the value. Prior to Proposition 13, this same homeowner was paying well over three times that amount annually in taxes.

Adapting to the spotlight of fame and success as readily as a duck takes to water, the curmudgeonly Howard Jarvis found himself besieged for his personal endorsement by politicians from both ends of the political spectrum. In one of the oddest political flip-flops ever, Governor Jerry Brown, who had been opposed to Proposition 13 prior to its enactment, suddenly embraced Howard Jarvis physically in public and announced, "Proposition 13 represents a great opportunity. We have our marching orders from the people. This is the strongest expression of the democratic process in a decade. Things will never be the same."

Political cartoonists lost no time in lampooning the governor as a born-again political specimen whom they christened, "Jerry Jarvis," while the real Mr. Jarvis responded to Brown's about-face by endorsing him for reelection in November. When California Republicans learned of Jarvis's endorsement of Brown, they were outraged. How could Jarvis do such a thing? He was supposed to be one of them. Hadn't the Republican party labored long and hard and helped him raise money to get the initiative on the ballot? Jarvis listened carefully and decided they had a point. He decided to fix things up in his own inimitable fashion. He simply issued a second statement endorsing the Republican candidate Evelle Younger for governor, too, without repudiating his endorsement of Brown. Now they both had his blessing. That should make everyone happy, no?

Predictably, the political marriage of Howard Jarvis and Paul Gann did not survive beyond the passage of Proposition 13. When Jarvis started receiving most of the publicity, Paul Gann denounced his erstwhile bedfellow as "irrational." "He has diarrhea of the mouth, and he has a very difficult time with the English language. It's hard for him to get above a two-letter word. He says *I* and *me* very well, though. Howard tried to climb the tree all his life and never succeeded. He was an utter failure until Proposition 13."

Not one to suffer such criticism in silence, Jarvis delivered a broadside of his own. "Unlike Gann, I was a successful businessman, and I didn't go into tax reform in a desperate attempt to find a way to earn a living. I could have bought and sold Paul Gann any day in the last half century. I spent sixteen years of my life fighting for tax reduction, long before Gann knew what that meant. He was a Johnny-come-lately who arrived on the scene after I and the other members of the United Organization of Taxpayers had done all the heavy work. We would have won with or without Paul Gann. But because I invited him to join us, he was able to share in the limelight. If I had not extended that invitation to him, nobody would ever have heard of Paul Gann."

What it came down to in the end was that the media seized upon Howard Jarvis because, quite simply, he was excellent copy. He was a caricature of himself, a genuine American folk hero.

The immediate result of Proposition 13 was a 10 percent reduction in local budgets throughout the state. The state government, which enjoyed a surplus of some $5 billion in its own coffers, thanks (ironically enough) to escalating property taxes during the preceding years, was able to soften the blow with an emergency bail-out bill totaling $4.3 billion. Because of the state's solvency, the economic disaster that critics of Proposition 13 had predicted prior to its enactment was avoided.

Most of the bail-out money went into the educational system, while another major portion went into a special fund to help local agencies meet acute cash shortages. The rest of the money was allocated evenly among the various county, city, and district governments. One of the most beneficial effects of Proposition 13, according to its sponsors, was an increase in "user fees" for public services for those who benefited most from them. For example, landing fees at airports, greens fees at municipal golf courses, docking fees for boat owners, admission fees at public swimming pools, racetracks, zoos, parks, theaters, and museums, and charges for other public facilities all went up to help take up the slack. Previously, most of these costs had been subsidized by property taxes. Jarvis and his colleagues had argued all along that golfers, tennis players, boat owners, and so forth ought to pay for their own amusements.

The success of Proposition 13 in California paved the way for similar legislation in other states where antitax fever was mounting. Voters in Alabama, Arizona, Hawaii, Idaho, Illinois, Missouri, Nevada, North and South Dakota, Texas, and Massachusetts had a chance to consider tax limitation and public spending bills shortly afterward. Robert Kuttner made the point in *Revolt of the Haves* that Proposition 13 fever is merely a continuation of the rebellion that has existed in American society throughout our history. Ohio passed the Smith Law, which is almost identical to Proposition 13, following a public uprising over high taxes in 1910. The voters in Rhode Island limited state taxing powers in an 1870 referendum. By and large, however, these were scattered instances occurring in areas where abuses were especially painful. The current tax rebellion, resulting in a nation-wide uprising against high taxes of all sorts and an underground economy creeping ever closer to the trillion dollar mark, has assumed the proportions of a full-scale revolution—a nonviolent revolution, but a revolution nonetheless.

Don Feder—The Architect of Proposition 2½

Just when it seemed as though the momentum generated by Proposition 13 was coming to a halt and the much heralded tax revolution of the late 1970s was being replaced once again by public apathy, voters in Massachusetts shocked the nation in 1980 with the passage of Proposition 2½. The Massachusetts law, while not quite as far-reaching as the one spawned by Jarvis and Gann, was nevertheless a radical measure in a state that had earned the onerous distinction of being the most heavily taxed state in the country many years before. Proposition 2½ limited the state's property tax to 2½ percent of market value. It also limited the the rate of growth in taxes to 2½ percent a year, and it had a rider that cut the state's rather steep auto excise tax in half.

The architect of Proposition 2½ was an intense young lawyer named Don Feder, the executive director of a conservative organization called Citizens for Limited Taxation. Feder, who had been active in political action groups since he was a student in the late 1960s, was another ardent disciple of Ayn Rand. The Randian philosophy maintains that the only legitimate function of government is national defense and the preservation of the peace. All other public institutions, such as schools, hospitals, museums, libraries, welfare, sanitation, fire, and so forth should be turned over to private enterprise. Throughout the 1970s Feder had been preaching the Randian message and disseminating his innumerable pamphlets and articles with the singlemindedness of a young missionary out to convert the heathen masses. But it wasn't until he struck upon the antitax theme in a state where people were literally screaming for relief that he was able to reach an audience beyond his own limited circles.

Suddenly, Don Feder had attracted the attention of some of the most powerful and well-financed business organizations in the state, including the Associated Industries of Massachusetts (the manufacturers' trade association) and the High Technology Council (representing the rapidly growing electronics and computer industries). Both these organizations, which had been lukewarm toward Feder's proposition in the past, jumped aboard the bandwagon and lent money and support to the cause. Proposition 2½ resulted in a sharp rollback of property taxes throughout the state, but the ax fell most heavily on the city of Boston, which taxed property above 6 percent of market value. Unlike California, the state treasury did not have the luxury of a substantial cash surplus to soften the blow.

Ironically enough, Proposition 2½, the most conservative antitax measure on the various state ballots in November, 1980, passed by a 3 to 2 margin in perhaps the most liberal state in the nation, while less drastic legislation failed in more conservative states such as Arizona, Nebraska, Nevada, Ohio, South Dakota, and Utah. Similar initiatives were approved by voters in Arkansas, Missouri, Montana, and West Virginia. Antitax leaders across the country argued that the legislation was enacted in the states where it was needed the most, while opponents claimed that the results were mixed and didn't signify any sort of decisive trend.

Estimates of the cuts mandated by Proposition 2½ ranged from 10 percent in some of the small, rural communities to 75 percent in urban areas, including Boston, which relied heavily on property taxes to finance their myriad public services. The state-wide average property tax, however, was 3.4 percent of market value, which translated into a 26 percent rollback overall. Obviously, the cities would be affected most severely.

Dire predictions of drastic reductions in police, fire, and sanitation services made the rounds throughout the state, a verbatim replay of the near hysteria that had gripped California two years earlier. Financial analysts warned that Boston might be forced to default on its bonds as New York City had done on its notes in 1976. Welfare payments to the poor might have to be curtailed, medical services eliminated, housing subsidies cut to the bone. The result would be an army of hungry and homeless outcasts roaming the streets. Liberals were careful, however, not to blame the voters of the state for the mess, but rather unresponsive politicians who had overburdened homeowners with high taxes rather than imposing unpopular new taxes to raise money.

"The two most extreme tax initiatives, Proposition 13 and Proposition 2½, were votes against property taxes that had gone out of control," Robert Kuttner admitted after the results were in.

"Taxes are so unbelievably high there that we wrote the state off," said a spokesman for the American Federation of State, County and Municipal Employees, explaining why his organization failed to campaign against the initiative in Massachusetts.

The fear campaign grew more and more strident as 1980 ground to a close. Politicians throughout the state referred to Proposition 2½ as "Apocalypse Now," and they spoke of tossing "hundreds of thousands of municipal workers" off the payrolls. In addition to policemen, firemen, and sanitation workers, "school teachers, sports coaches, school-bus drivers, meter maids, park-maintenance workers, street sweepers, office clerks, and secretaries" would all lose their jobs.

"Fountains won't be spouting water on Boston Common any more," warned a councilman from Boston. "Schools, parks, and beaches will be closed. Lights will be shut off at gyms, athletic fields, and tennis courts. High school sports will become a thing of the past. Schoolchildren living less than two miles from school will have to walk. Potholes will remain unfilled."

The councilman, who chose to remain anonymous, did not explain why children would have to walk to schools that were going to be closed anyway, according to him, or why potholes remained unfilled even before Proposition 2½ went into effect.

The police chief of Foxboro lamented that his patrolmen would have to do without their one-dog canine corps and might even have to put the old mongrel to rest if they couldn't afford to feed him. The city of Quincy issued a statement that it might have to shut down all eight of its elementary schools and fire the city's 226 public school teachers.

Through all the wailing and gnashing of teeth, the unflappable Don Feder refused to lose his composure. "If people were happy with their police protection, the quality of education their children were receiving, and all the other services government has been providing, they wouldn't have voted for 2½ in the first place," he said without hesitation. Like Howard Jarvis two years earlier, Don Feder was in the right place at the right time with the right message. His time, after more than a decade of intensive proselytizing, had finally arrived.

While the full impact of Propositions 13, 2½, and similar tax-reduction legislation will not be known for several years, there is no question that it will change the way that state and local governments manage the public purse.

"If this is fully implemented as planned over the next two years, we will not have the money to pay for one single city employee after paying off annual debts on bonds and other fixed costs," said James Sullivan, the city manager of Cambridge, Massachusetts, which stood to lose one third of its tax revenues after the 1980 election. "We will have to lay off one-third of our employees—that's 250 teachers, 100 firemen, 100 policemen, 175 public works employees—and we'll have to close down the health clinics, the branch libraries, the community schools. And that's just the first year."

When various municipal officials prevailed upon Governor Edward J. King to raise other taxes to help make up some of the difference, King refused to accommodate them. "I don't think when the voters expressed themselves that they were saying, let's cut taxes here and increase them in another section, so that the total taxation will remain the same," he said.

Citizens for Limited Taxation was quick to remind the governor of the voters' mandate. The attorney for the organization, George S. Hyatt, issued a statement suggesting, "There'll be a lot of caterwauling by the voters if the legislature tries to frustrate their intent."

With all the furor over the "drastic cuts" mandated by the new law, Hyatt and his associates promised to fight for even deeper tax reductions in the future. Taxes were so high in Massachusetts, they said, that even after the passage of Proposition 2½, property taxes throughout the state would remain 25 percent higher than the national average of 2 percent of market value.

The States Suffer, but the Rebellion Still Grows

Meanwhile, three years after the adoption of Proposition 13 in California, Governor Jerry Brown prepared to face the new fiscal year without the luxury of a cash surplus to fall back on. The $5 billion surplus of 1978 had just run out as Brown faced a battery of reporters early in 1981 and announced, "The moment of truth is upon us."

His budget proposal for fiscal 1982 was $24.5 billion, a mere $300 million increase from the previous year. Compounding his problem was a recent reduction in the state's income tax, which had also gotten to be a source of irritation among California taxpayers. Lower income taxes would result in an estimated reduction in tax revenues of $2 billion, on top of the $7 billion-a-year loss in property taxes. There was no question, said Brown, but that the state would have to restrict pay increases for public employees and reduce welfare and medical allotments to local governments. He also threatened to repeal cost-of-living raises for welfare mothers and the handicapped.

In addition to Massachusetts and California, Ohio was forced to cut back on a laundry list of services because of recently enacted antitax laws. The state's school budget was reduced substantially, resulting in the shutdown of several schools, and officials projected a $500 million deficit for the coming fiscal year.

Governor Albert H. Quie of Minnesota claimed that he was trimming the state's welfare rolls "in a loving and caring way" because of an impending $1 billion deficit mandated by the tax revolution in his state. Irate voters had fought for and won nearly $800 million worth of cuts in both income and property taxes.

In the northeast, Connecticut's new governor, William A. O'Neill, told the legislature in Hartford, "It seems we have only one choice: curb spending and control taxation." Liberal Democrats in the state had long been lobbying for a state income tax to close a projected $200 million budget deficit, but O'Neill, himself a Democrat and political ally of his deceased predecessor, Ella Grasso, remained adamant in his opposition to the income tax. Voters throughout the state, he said, were already up in arms over the state's extremely high 7½ percent sales tax, as well as relatively high personal property taxes.

Some of the more solvent states, such as Arizona, which had eliminated its sales tax on food, and Texas, which was contemplating a $1 billion property tax cut, were better able to cope with losses in state revenues. But even here, financial crunches were anticipated not too far down the road. While all these tax and expenditure reductions were taking place in the states that had already been socked by antitax legislation, other areas of the nation were gearing up for tax rebellions of their own.

The revolution, it seemed, was just getting started.

Advocates of additional tax reductions on federal, state, and local levels interpreted the results of the tax rebellion differently, however. Governor Jerry Brown of California was creating a phony crisis, charged an editorial writer for *The Wall Street Journal*. Despite Brown's claim that he would have to "repeal cost-of-living raises for welfare mothers, the blind, and the handicapped," the editorial made the point that his proposed new budget of $24.5 billion was "one and three-quarters times as large as the last state budget before Messrs. Jarvis and Gann started the Proposition 13 revolution in June, 1978. The average annual increase works out to 18.8 percent, pretty healthy by any standard."

The implication here is that Brown deliberately used up his huge surplus to beef up spending in order to create a "crisis" later on.

The newspaper went on to state that, Proposition 13 notwithstanding, assessed property values grew by nearly 18 percent in fiscal 1981, producing more than $700 million in extra property tax revenues for the state, enough to offset Brown's threatened rollback in welfare payments to the poor. The state and local governments hired back nearly all the civil employees they fired in the aftermath of Proposition 13, claimed *The Wall Street Journal*. In addition, California's private economy benefited substantially from the tax reduction, with lower unemployment and many new jobs made available in the private sector. All indicators pointed to recurring surpluses rather than scarcity in coming years, the editorial said, thanks to a lower tax burden mandated by Proposition 13. "Reducing tax rates now sets the stage for stronger revenue growth in the future."

This, basically, is the supply-side economic argument made by many of the young advisers surrounding President Ronald Reagan: lower taxes, they say, will strengthen the economy and generate more revenue for the government than will confiscatory taxes, which lead to recession.

One of the primary objectives of tax-cut proponents is, of course, the transfer of jobs from the public to the private sector. The public sector has grown too large, the argument goes, with fewer and fewer private employees paying higher and higher taxes to finance a gargantuan bureaucracy. Toward this end, Propositions 13, 2½, and other tax-reduction initiatives would appear to be at least initially successful.

"Recent data seem to portend the end of the explosive growth in state and local spending that has been with us for decades," said Rudolph G. Penner, a former assistant director for economic policy in President Ford's Office of Management and Budget. Between 1949 and 1977, Penner claims, state and local spending rose from 7.8 to 14.3 percent of the gross national product while federal spending went from 15.2 to 18.6 percent of GNP. On a per capita basis, state and local spending soared 266 percent in the same period *after adjusting for inflation.*

Since 1978, however, the growth rate of state and local spending has declined significantly, and the staff of the Advisory Commission on Intergovernmental Relations is now looking forward to an actual decrease in real per capita spending during the next few years. While Penner does not attribute this exclusively to the new American tax revolution, he does expect the growing antitax militancy to be a major factor in reducing the size of the public monolith.

The leaders of the various tax protest groups have every intention of stepping up their activities in the months and years ahead, despite all the forecasts of "Apocalypse Now" by politicians across the country.

"Doesn't all this talk of shutting down schools and putting police and firemen out to pasture concern you at all?" I asked Don Feder, who is now the director of the Second Amendment Foundation, an anti-gun control group based in Bellevue, Washington.

"Politicians always threaten to cut the most vital and popular services first to frighten the public. They never talk about waste and fraud."

"Is there any chance they can overturn Proposition 2½ in Massachusetts?"

"One of the provisions of 2½ is that cities and towns can exempt themselves with a two-thirds vote by the public. They're not locked in forever if they decide they don't want it."

"So the politicians are trying to frighten the public into tossing it out is what you're saying."

"They always use demagoguery to get what they want. They won't get away with it, though. This revolution hasn't even started yet."

*   *   *

Jim Davidson, Howard Jarvis, Don Feder, and other leaders of the mainstream tax protest organizations all expect to maintain busy schedules during the coming years.

One of the fastest growing of these groups is the National Tax Limitation Committee (NTLC), which was founded in 1975 by Lewis Uhler, a former activist for the John Birch Society and antipoverty director for Ronald Reagan when he was governor of California; William Rickenbacker, a financial adviser and columnist for William F. Buckley's *National Review*; and a group of conservative businessmen and economists, including Nobel Prize winner Milton Friedman.

The NTLC is campaigning for a constitutional amendment that would limit government spending to a fixed percentage of the gross national product. This measure is regarded as less severe than Jim Davidson's amendment to balance the budget, and it has the backing of many Republicans and economic advisers to the Reagan administration. What this all adds up to are increased efforts by a variety of organizations to limit the taxing power of government, cut back on expenditures, and generally reduce the size of the public sector while stimulating private initiative.

The Underground Economy continues to grow and prosper, and the army of illegal tax protesters and revolutionaries is likewise expanding from year to year. But much of this radicalism has now surfaced and worked its way into the mainstream, legal structure of the nation's institutions. As a result, the revolution has gained a measure of respectability among the legions of hard-working, law-abiding, middle-class taxpayers. Millions of these Americans participate, to one extent or another, in the multi-billion-dollar underground economy, which has now grown to epidemic proportions.

We'll take a closer look now at this vast, secret netherside of the American economy.

—————— CHAPTER THREE ——————

The Underground Economy

The $700 Billion Underground Economy— A Reaction to Economic Recklessness and Government Ineptitude

While Ronald Reagan promised to fill his budget-cutting staff with people who were "meaner than a junkyard dog" when he assumed the presidency in January 1980, battle-scarred veterans of the fiscal foxholes warned that they had heard it all before. Every new president, including Jimmy Carter, promises a war on waste, fraud, and abuse in government spending, only to get lost in the impenetrable jungle of the federal bureaucracy a short time later. The American public, frustrated by decades of unfulfilled promises, soaring inflation, and rising taxes, decided long ago to conduct its own private war on fiscal irresponsibility. Tired of waiting for their elected representatives to do the job for them, the American people have taken matters into their own hands.

An estimated 20 to 30 million working Americans participate in the underground economy of the United States by hiding all or a significant portion of their income from the federal government each year.

Sylvia Porter describes this phenomenon in the following manner: "A veiled economy more vast in scope than most of the individual economies of most of the other countries on this globe lies underneath the in-the-open economy in which tens of millions of us in the United States live. An immense proportion of all the transactions that occur in our country take place in this underground—but they are untraced in any fashion, thus uncounted, unreported and most significant, untaxed. You yourself may well be a part of it, without even being aware that you are."

With this last sentence, Ms. Porter is being perhaps a bit too ingenuous; it is a safe bet that most people who fail to report income to IRS know exactly what they are doing and why they are doing it.

Mortimer Caplin, the IRS Commissioner under John F. Kennedy and Lyndon Johnson, maintains that "if merely a small portion of the income flowing through the underground—the legal portion—were taxed at minimum rates, the 1981 federal budget deficit easily could be balanced."

Yet William E. Williams, the deputy commissioner of the IRS in 1981, admits that "tax cheaters are getting away with it (1) in increasing numbers and (2) on a mounting scale." He warned, however, that IRS was preparing "far more severe programs" to collect taxes on this income during the struggle ahead.

Some of the methods people have been utilizing to avoid taxes include barter arrangements whereby individuals exhange services (a dentist, for example, provides $1,000 worth of work for a carpenter's family in trade for $1,000 worth of improvements on the dentist's office) without money changing hands; cash payments for babysitting services or maintenance and repair work by plumbers and electricians with no records sent to the IRS; unreported tips to waiters and taxi drivers; profit-skimming by people who have cash businesses, such as doctors, lawyers, retailers, and owners of mom-and-pop operations; unreported capital gains from the sale of securities, real estate, and other valuables; unreported rent and royalty income by property owners and freelance professionals; unreported interest and dividend income, which Caplin estimates to be as much as 16 percent of the total. All this is legal income and doesn't include the billions of dollars made each year through clandestine activities such as drug peddling, gambling, loansharking, pimping and prostitution, and other criminal operations.

In 1981 the IRS collected close to $550 billion in taxes on reported income of approximately $2.5 trillion. Estimated unreported income in the United States ranges between $500 billion and $700 billion a year, with some analysts suggesting that it may soon be as much as a trillion dollars. What this means is that, for every four dollars of legal income reported to the government each year, there is another one dollar hidden from view. Illegal income is, naturally enough, totally unreported, and comprises a separate underworld economy in itself.

Why has an underground economy of such immense proportions emerged in the United States of America which is, quite possibly, the freest and most open society on earth today? The reasons given by tax protesters and critics of tax cheating alike are remarkably similar. Those who have studied the situation from both points of view agree that the main causes of taxpayer revolt today are inflation, which squeezes people on the one side with constantly rising prices and on the other with higher tax brackets that are not indexed for inflation; disgust with scandal, waste, and outright thievery involving public officials;

a growing awareness of the limited capabilities of the IRS's enforcement arm despite warnings to the contrary; the recurrence of monstrous federal and state budget deficits that are an invitation to the individual taxpayer to live beyond his own means; and the sheer complexity of the tax laws themselves, which have been known to drive even financial experts to the brink of drooling imbecility.

Step One—Taking Cash to the Laundry

One of the federal government's main concerns is that the American people, who have traditionally been among the most law-abiding people on earth, are now breaking the law in increasing numbers where taxes are concerned. More important than anything else is the fact that these same law-abiding citizens, who consider other types of illegal behavior unpatriotic, have no qualms whatsoever about concealing income from the IRS.

"Stealing from a thief is no crime at all. Hell, I'm performing a patriotic duty by keeping the money where it'll do the most good: right here in my own pocket. I can put it back to work in my business instead of turning it over to the crooks at IRS. That's what free enterprise is all about. That's what keeps the economy going," an avowed participant in the underground economy said to me recently. His sentiments are repeated over and over in similar language by hundreds of people across the country when they discuss their own personal war against the IRS.

"My best clients are *not* the executives of big corporations who are knocking down seventy or eighty grand a year," said a stockbroker for a major brokerage house in April 1981. "These guys have half their income taken out before they even see their checks. Most of them are living comfortably, to be sure, but they're in hock up to their eyeballs in order to increase their deductions, and they have very little discretionary income to invest. No, my best clients are the ones with cash businesses, restaurant and bar owners, shopkeepers, plumbers, electricians, doctors, dentists, you name it. They're the ones with all the cash. They pay themselves a salary, say $20,000 a year from their corporation, and they're skimming maybe another $500 a week which goes right into a safe deposit box. I can't tell you how many of these people come to me and say, 'Hey, I've got to get rid of some cash. I have $30,000 I've got to hide somewhere. What can you do for me?'"

"What *do* you do for them? Is there a standard way to launder that kind of money?"

"It's not my job to ask nosy questions. The less I know, the better off I am. So I tell them their legal rights. They can bring in up to $10,000 dollars at a time without brokerage firms or banks having to report it to IRS. $9,999 is okay, $10,000 has to be reported."

"How often can they do this?"

"There's no hard and fixed rule on this. The law says, if they bring in cash on a regular basis, we're supposed to report it as soon as it goes over ten grand. Actually, it's up to the discretion of each institution. If somebody's coming in once a month like clockwork with a bag full of cash, chances are he's going to be reported just to cover ourselves. But if it's irregular, $6,000 today, $8,000 three months from now, $7,000 nine months later, he should be all right. Generally speaking, an individual is better off bringing it in only once a year to *ten different* places.

There's no coordination among the banks and brokerage houses to keep track of it all."

"What's the usual way of investing this cash? These people are looking for privacy, no doubt."

"Unquestionably, most of this money, 95 percent of it, goes into bearer bonds. No record of the transaction is reported to the government. And since the client takes possession of the bonds, there are no records of interest payments to be reported either."

"You're talking about municipals, right?"

"Municipals and Treasuries. A lot of people don't realize it, but you can get Treasuries in bearer form, too, and they pay higher interest."

"The interest on municipals is legally tax-free. How about treasury bond interest?"

"You're supposed to report that and pay federal tax on it, but it's exempt from state and city taxes."

"But how does the government know who's collecting interest on bearer bonds if there's no record of the payments?"

"The answer is, the government doesn't have the foggiest notion who's collecting what. Treasury bearer bonds are one of the best deals around today for somebody looking to hide money from Uncle Sam. The average guy is not aware of them, but sophisticated investors have been getting away with it for years."

"But the government's not stupid. Why doesn't it just stop issuing bonds in bearer form?"

The broker's face broke into a wide smile as he replied, "That's the best part of all. Uncle Sam *can't afford* to stop issuing bearer bonds. Uncle Sam has to keep on borrowing money just to stay in business. One way the government gets people to invest in Treasuries instead of triple-A corporates, which pay higher interest, is by issuing bearer certificates."

"So what you're saying is that, in reality, the government is making it easy for people to cheat. It's practically encouraging tax evasion."

"You got it. If the federal government stopped issuing bearer bonds tomorrow, it would dry up a major source of its own revenue."

Because of its nature, the underground economy is difficult, if not impossible, to measure accurately. The IRS, in an effort to downplay the phenomenon, estimates unreported income to be approximately 7 percent of GNP, or $250 billion. Independent analysts, however, say that a more accurate figure is as much as 20 percent of GNP. More significant than the current dollar volume, say the experts, is the fact that the underground economy has grown at twice the rate of the regular economy during the past decade. These figures are supported by Peter M. Gutmann, a City University of New York professor of economics, and Edgar L. Feige, a University of Wisconsin economist, who have done the most serious work to date in studying and analyzing the underground economy.

"There are tremendous policy implications to the Underground Economy," said Charles J. Haulk, senior business economist at the Federal Reserve Bank in Atlanta, during a 1981 interview. "Unemployment is undoubtedly overstated because the work force is being better utilized than the traditional measures would indicate. As a result, fiscal and monetary policy tends to be too stimulative, which, in turn, increases inflation."

According to statistics compiled by the IRS, certain types of people are more likely than others to hide portions of their income, and their returns will be more carefully scrutinized in the future. These types include self-employed professionals, farmers, small business people, lawyers, doctors, dentists, accountants, shopkeepers, and household servants. IRS computers estimate that these people are reporting only about 60 percent of their real income and hiding the rest.

"There's no question that people are becoming more aggressive about taking deductions," said Ellen Murphy, a public information officer for the IRS, in the spring of 1981.

"One of the problems is that more people are learning how to dodge taxes, so more of them are doing it," admitted an IRS agent based in New York City.

"How?"

"It's bad enough it's going on," he replied. "I have no intention of giving people lessons."

Cash Receipts and Other Untraceable Incomes

Lessons on how to evade taxes are not required by most people, it seems; the public has apparently discovered all the available schemes on its own.

"I found a foolproof scheme," said the voice on the other end of the phone.

"What is it?" I asked.

"An employment agency. It can't miss. Guaranteed profits. You should see them. Every Monday they line up out in the hall looking for jobs. You'd think I was giving away free hotcakes. All I do is rent an office and hang out a shingle: Employment Agency. I put an ad in the *Daily News* and wait for them to line up."

"But what's the angle? You don't get paid unless you find them work, and then it's by check from a company, right?"

"Not me. I'm different. I specialize in minorities."

"How's that?"

"Puerto Ricans, Haitians, people who can't read English. I got all the jobs for them."

"You've got the jobs? Where?"

"That's the gimmick, see? I clip the jobs right out of the newspaper. These people *can't read.* So I just clip the ads, they pay me $50 cash money right on the table, and I send them out to get the jobs. I'm on the books for $200 a week, and another four or five bills a week goes right in my pocket."

"That's . . . that's incredible."

"It's guaranteed, like hotcakes. I'm gonna open a branch in all the ghettos. You want to be my partner?"

While this operation is marginal at best, skirting a fine line between sleazy opportunism and outright fraud, millions of legitimate, hard-working entrepreneurs throughout the country are no less imaginative than he is in their efforts to hide income from Uncle Sam.

A financial executive with a major corporation decided that a Manhattan brownstone would be an ideal investment for himself. In addition to appreciating substantially in value over the years, the brownstone would provide him with cash flow in the form of rent from his various tenants, as well as a tax shelter through depreciation of his property and deductions for interest payments, taxes, and maintenance costs. His job brings in a salary of over $50,000 a year, and the income from his property amounts to another $23,000 annually. However, $8,000 of this rental income goes into his own pocket, untaxed, while $15,000 is reported to IRS.

How does the young executive get away with this? Quite simply, by giving his tenants a discount on their rent and telling them to make their checks out to cash, a transaction which is virtually impossible for the IRS to trace.

"Of course, when I hire people I insist on paying them with a personal check," he said with a smile. "You want to be able to prove your expenses and hide your income. That's the whole game."

On the other side of town, the owner of a chic bar and restaurant admitted, "A small business like this is one of the great ways to cheat Uncle Sam."

How?

The restaurateur reports about 75 percent of his total revenues and tucks the balance away in a safe deposit box. "I keep two cash registers," he said. "One upstairs in plain view, and another one in my back office. The one upstairs is just for show." An IRS agent or investigator who was "spotting" his store (that is, spying on him while pretending to be a customer) would ascertain that he was indeed ringing up every drink and meal. But he would have no way of knowing that the bar owner used a phony tape from the register in his back office when making out his tax return.

Accountants, too, have been known to cooperate with their clients in falsifying tax returns—for a high fee, of course. The head of a small advertising firm based in the Midwest claimed that he finally got rid of his tax accountant because "the guy was just too much for me. I was losing sleep at night with visions of my wife and kids bringing me cookies in jail."

"What was he doing for you?"

"Just about everything you can imagine. Changing the dates on checks, claiming my wife as a business deduction, manufacturing vouchers for trips I never took and meals I never ate. I was a nervous wreck, so I got rid of him.

"Still, there are people I know who swear by the guy. Apparently he's been getting away with it for years."

Off-the-books second jobs are another major source of undeclared income for a growing number of people. The International Labor Organization (ILO), an agency of the United Nations, reported recently that, according to its own studies, one of every four workers in the United States and Canada holds a secret second job. According to the ILO, this phenomenon is not limited to North America alone. Italy has, perhaps, more second-job holders than any country on earth, with 65 percent of its public employees working secretly in the private sector and entire factories specializing in shoe and clothing manufacturing staffed by off-the-books workers. West Germany and France are not too far behind; both countries are losing billions of dollars a year in untaxed revenues, and even supposedly law-abiding Sweden has a growing underground economy that rivals that of its European neighbors.

"It's easy to find a second job that pays you off the books anywhere in the world," an illegal alien in the United States who has held jobs throughout Europe at different times admitted in an interview.

A spokesman for the ILO stated that there is "a highly efficient system of work force trafficking in the U.S. and Europe," finding jobs for illegal immigrants. The numbers amount to over three hundred thousand illegal workers in West Germany, and as many as 6 million in the United States. It is unlikely that this trend will be reversed without the "reduction or at least the stabilization of taxation and social security charges," the ILO study reported.

The availability of counterfeit social security cards in the United States makes it virtually impossible for illegal job holders to be identified. Maria Gangadeen, an alien from Guyana with a temporary visa, testified before a federal grand jury in New York that she was able to obtain a fake social security card for eighty dollars from a man dressed as a priest who called himself "Father Robert." Phony social security cards are also used by American citizens who have a legal declared job under their own name and who moonlight off-the-books with their counterfeit cards.

Besides failing to report income received in the underground economy, many people have found it relatively easy to qualify for welfare payments while they hold secret jobs. Government comes out a double loser in these cases; it loses the revenue from the untaxed secret income, and it is actually paying out welfare money to those who don't qualify for it.

Most of these cases go undetected each year, resulting in the loss of many billions of dollars in untaxed secret income. Maria Gangadeen, the alien from Guyana, decided to testify to the federal grand jury, however, when she tried to buy a birth certificate as well as a social security card from "Father Robert" and his partner, "Father John." It seems the two gentlemen had the audacity to offend the young woman's sensibilities during the second transaction.

"Father John asked me where I wanted to be born," she said, "and I jocularly told him Atlanta. But I was too embarrassed to use the birth certificate because it described me as the out-of-wedlock daughter of a North Carolina tobacco worker and a Georgia housemaid."

Fathers "Robert" and "John" had clearly gone too far. Their little joke offended Ms. Gangadeen's pride and earned them a lengthy stay in a federal penitentiary.

Trying to determine how many of the 270 million

social security cards floating around this country are being used illegally is a monumental task, to say the least. Every now and then federal agents break up a counterfeiting ring involving huge quantities of fraudulent cards. In 1979 six people were indicted in Los Angeles for issuing about seven thousand cards to illegal aliens between 1975 and 1978. Four of the defendants, including a retired police officer, a court reporter, and a Social Security Administration employee, were sent to jail, but the other two jumped bail and are fugitives in Mexico, it is believed.

The seven thousand cards in question, however, were only the tip of the iceberg. During the trial, three of the defendants testified that they had processed a total of eighty thousand phony social security cards for aliens at a charge of $15 apiece. And this is only one operation out of dozens operating illegally throughout the country. How many false cards are in existence today, in addition to the known 270 million issued by Social Security, is anybody's guess.

During the past few years, a few people in government have been talking about replacing the old social security card with a new supercard featuring a color photograph of the holder and pertinent information regarding sex and birth date that could be read electronically. This idea has been proposed by Father Theodore Hesburgh, president of Notre Dame University, who was the chairman of the Select Commission on Immigration and Refugee Policy in 1981.

But civil libertarians remain adamantly opposed to any kind of "Orwellian national identity card." "This card would be just another way to discriminate against Hispanics, Asians, and any other minority group that happens to be coming into the counrty," objected Arnold Torres, a lobbyist for the League of

Latin American Citizens, while testifying before a Senate subcommittee.

Other critics contend that the new cards would cost billions of dollars to administer and police, and they would be just as vulnerable to fraud as the old cards.

"At the moment, the mood of the Congress would make it difficult to win support for a more elaborate social security card," said Republican Senator Alan Simpson of Wyoming, the chairman of the Senate subcommittee on Immigration and Refugee Policy, in the spring of 1981.

The Cash-Free Barter Exchange

Dealing in cash. Undeclared tips. Skimming profits. Keeping two sets of books. Failing to report freelance income and capital gains transactions. Moonlighting off-the-books. These are all commonly used methods of hiding income from IRS and participating in the underground economy.

And then there is barter.

Barter transactions, according to new studies, may well be the fastest-growing sector of the underground economy today. No less a personage than Albert Einstein declared shortly before his death, "If I had my life to live over again, I would elect to be a trader of goods rather than a student of science. I think barter is a noble thing."

Barter, which is nothing more or less than the exchange of goods and services without money changing hands, is as old as mankind. Indeed, the use of money as a medium of exchange did not enter the human experience until quite some time after the first humanoids started swapping food, clothing, weapons, and other valuables among themselves. Barter has been with us for tens of thousands of years, and, while it was necessary to invent money as a measure of value in order to develop a dynamic, complex economic system, barter, on a limited scale at least, continues to provide us with social and economic benefits today. In fact, the age of the computer has elevated the art of bartering to a level no one even imagined possible a short while ago.

The trading of goods and services has always been popular among individuals, but in recent years an entire barter industry has emerged, with major corporations as well as individuals transacting hundreds of millions of dollars worth of business each year. There are an estimated four to five hundred trade exchanges or barter clubs flourishing in the United States at this moment. The number and quality of these exchanges is increasing rapidly as more and more people transact a good percentage of their annual business in the underground economy.

The dilemma this poses for the IRS rests in the fact that it regards all this barter business as taxable income, as though the goods and services had been paid for with money. If a dentist does $1,000 worth of work for a carpenter in return for the carpenter's improvements on his office, IRS would like to tax both individuals on $1,000 each in extra income. IRS considers the dentist and the carpenter to have received "payments in kind at fair market value." Had the dental and carpentry work been paid for in cash, each man would have had to report this income on his tax return for the year. But since the services were bartered or traded for each other, with no records kept and sent to the IRS, it is difficult if not impossible for the IRS to tax this income accordingly. Multiply this simple transaction by hundreds of thousands of others engaged in each year, not only by individuals but by small and large corporations as well, and you begin to get some idea of the enormity of the situation.

Pfeister Barter, Inc., is a trade exchange that was established in New York City in 1978. Pfeister Barter has well over a thousand listed members ranging from retailers to small businesses and professional organizations. A typical transaction might involve a law firm that takes a client out to dinner at a restaurant that is also a member of the exchange. Instead of paying for the dinner in cash or putting it on a credit card, the law firm presents a blue-and-white barter card and has trade units deducted from its account at Pfeister. In effect, Pfeister is serving as a clearinghouse or a bank, a barter bank with members depositing trade units instead of cash in its computers.

Some time later, the owner of the restaurant may require legal services that will be provided by the law firm in exchange for the meal, or he might buy some other goods or services from another member with the trade units that have been deducted from the law firm's account and deposited in his own. In the latter instance, trade units are used as money to buy something from a third party, but at no time does money ever change hands. The various members of the club deposit goods and services with the exchange, which then evaluates each deposit at its fair market value and translates this into a corresponding number of trade units. Like any other broker or clearing house, Pfeister Barter charges a fee or a commission for its services; in addition to an annual membership fee, the buyer in each transaction pays Pfeister an 8 percent commission in the form of trade units. Pfeister then uses these trading units to buy whatever it needs—office space, furniture, typewriters—from other members of the exchange.

A representative of Pfeister Barter considers each

member's relationship with IRS his own personal business. "I would never ask if these transactions are reported to the IRS and I don't want to know," he said. "It's not our role to advise people on the tax treatment of these transactions."

One of the four principals behind Barter Systems of Southern Connecticut, Inc., expressed a bit more concern about the IRS's attitude toward his own organization.

"We expect to be audited heavily by IRS," he said in response to my question. "When members ask me if we report all their transaction to IRS I tell them candidly, 'Not at present, but this could change at any time in the future.' We are not advocating that people participate in the underground economy, and I think that's a dangerous thing. We're in this business because there's a definite need for barter and it provides real economic benefits to everyone involved. What each member reports to IRS is his own business. But I intend to open my books fully to IRS whenever they ask. We're right out in the open about everything."

Barter Systems of Southern Connecticut is a division of Barter Systems, Inc., which is headquartered in Oklahoma City. Barter Systems arranged well over $100 million in barter business in 1981, and it expects to do substantially more in coming years. Its members include some of the major corporations in the country, including airline, energy, and industrial companies. One of its larger transactions involved the exchange of a jet airplane for $1.3 million worth of coal. On a more mundane scale, its newsletters are filled with ads by people looking to swap food, dog grooming, religious instruction, plumbing work, and an impressive array of similar items. The federal government itself has given its imprimatur to bartering as a way of life; in 1980 the Civil Aeronautics Board granted permission to the airlines to trade airline tickets for food, liquor, and other goods they use on their planes.

Barter Systems, Inc., opened for business in 1975 with two offices in Oklahoma, and today it has more than fifty franchises operating across the United States. Business has been so brisk that the parent company is able to charge more than $50,000 for a franchise license in choice areas of the country. David Dehlin, the owner of the West Houston franchise, is busy on the phone all day long exchanging belly dancing lessons for paid vacations, business forms for plumbing services, and dozens of other products to satisfy his members' needs. His volume surpassed $4 million in 1980, up from $250,000 in 1977, and he anticipates 20 percent annual growth in the future. One member alone, a wood specialty store, does $1,000 a month in barter business in addition to its cash sales. Through Barter Systems it has purchased office equipment, carpeting, various supplies, and the services of a bartender for an opening party, all without laying out a cent.

In Columbus, Ohio, a Ford dealer installed a $19,000 car wash in exchange for two automobiles. In Oklahoma City and in Stamford, Connecticut, barter showrooms display merchandise offered by various members so that prospective traders can browse and select items they would like to exchange for goods and services of their own. In order to counter the image of barter clubs as nothing more than a tax dodge, the industry has formed an organization called the International Association of Trade Exchanges (IATE) to establish standards for members.

"We want to police the industry strongly from within," said a representative of Barter Systems and a founder of IATE during a recent interview.

IATE now represents over a hundred barter clubs with fifty thousand members in every state in the country. An IATE lawyer admitted that "every time an example was raised of what the underground economy consisted of, the word *barter* was mentioned. It's important that the industry be on good footing in regard to taxes."

In trying to bend over backward to accommodate the IRS, however, the various trade exchanges have run into problems with some of their own members, who would rather keep their transactions private. Many members resent the publication of membership lists, and they admit off the record that beating the tax man is their main reason for joining a barter club in the first place.

"I might as well trade for cash if it's all going to be reported to Uncle Sam," said one barter club member. "There's no benefit without the secrecy."

A principal of Barter Systems of Southern Connecticut disagreed with this statement, however. "There's a definite economic advantage in barter even when it's reported to IRS," he said to me. "It brings people extra business they wouldn't ordinarily have. It also helps them move the inventory they're having trouble getting rid of. Barter saves them money, as well. The dealer who buys goods for $100 wants only one thing: he wants to sell them at retail for $200. When we send him a customer who buys his goods for 200 trade units, he's getting his retail price for merchandise he had trouble selling in the first place, and then he can trade those units for $200 worth of labor from an electrician, say, to fix up his store. In effect, that electrical work has cost him only $100 in cash—the actual cash he originally paid for his merchandise. Barter has enabled him to sell a difficult item, and it has made it possible for him to get $200 worth of work done for $100.

"That's why I'm not worried about losing members if we cooperate with IRS. There's a definite economic advantage to barter, and people recognize that fact."

A key officer of Atwood Richards, which did about $200 million in barter business in 1981, agreed. "Manufacturers' inventories are at an all-time high. It is too expensive to borrow nowadays, so it makes sense to use those swollen inventories instead of cash to pay for things."

Among the items he has received in exchange for "swollen inventories" of his own are hotel rooms, airline tickets, convention facilities, tennis rackets, dietary foods, bat manure, advertising time on television, digital clocks, and toiletries.

"There is always a market for a product at a price," he added. Barter will be with us, he said, as long as there are manufacturers with slow-moving products, the IRS notwithstanding.

On an international level, bartering has always existed among various nations, although they prefer to call these transactions by a different name for the sake of propriety. And so the world of international exchange has given rise to such arcane terms as *counterpurchases, compensation transactions, countertrade,* and *reciprocal contracts.* When you get right down to it, however, the different governments on planet Earth are doing nothing more or less than swapping with one another.

A third-world country with a cash shortage, for example, is forced to barter its natural resources in exchange for food and military hardware. The major powers think nothing of trading their own food surpluses for badly needed strategic metals. One of the classic barter arrangements involved Communist Bulgaria and the United States, two countries that do not have an official trade pact with each other. To get around this little political wrinkle, Bulgaria shipped zinc concentrate to Holland, where it was smelted into zinc metal in exchange for industrial goods. From there it was sent to Argentina, which then sent beef directly to the United States, which, in turn, sent Bulgaria the product they wanted in the first place: American computers.

Barter Systems, Inc., couldn't have done it better.

The Economy May Not be As Ill-Fed As It Looks

All this underground activity, besides posing a monumental headache for IRS and its army of tax collectors, is also causing distortions in the government's key economic indicators. Edger L. Feige, the University of Wisconsin economist mentioned earlier, estimated that "prices in the unobserved economy may be as much as 20 percent to 40 percent lower than in the observed sector," where prices reflect such additional costs as taxes. Unemployment figures, he added, are also exaggerated, since they do not take into consideration the secret jobs people are holding in the underground economy. Productivity, too, is higher in the underground economy, said Feige, because "the reward is higher per hour of work" when income is not taxed.

In other words, the overall economy of the United States may actually be a lot healthier than official figures indicate, with lower inflation, lower unemployment, and higher productivity reflected in the underground economy.

The danger rests in the fact, said Feige, that "the patient [that is, the official economy] believes herself to be sick, and this impression of serious dysfunction is continually reinforced by the swarms of academic, government, and journalistic economists mumbling crisis at her bedside." This leads "well-intentioned policy makers to overstimulate the economy" in such a way as to cause higher inflation in the above-ground economy and increase the potential for financial collapse.

Another negative result of the expanding underground economy, according to a study conducted by the Federal Reserve Bank of Atlanta, is that "a disproportionate share of the tax burden is borne by those who are not engaged in the Underground Economy." A vicious cycle has been set into motion: as workers in the above-ground economy are forced to shoulder a greater portion of the tax burden, more of them are tempted to hide income and participate in the underground economy.

The Atlanta Fed's study also concluded that the underground economy may well have tripled in relation to the GNP during the past ten years, putting its total dollar volume at around $700 billion a year, which corrseponds to the figure mentioned by Edgar Feige. If this is true, the underground economy of the United States is larger than the official gross national product of France.

It has been suggested that massive tax cuts might be the most sensible way for the government to defuse much of this subterranean economic activity. When Professor Peter M. Gutmann of the City University of New York testified before the Joint Economic Committee in November 1979, he asked rhetorically, "What is the theoretical tax loss involved in the subterranean economy? The upper IRS estimate is $26 billion for 1976. However, the IRS study team left out a number of categories and may have underestimated others. Once these omitted categories are added, the tax loss for 1976 will be more than $35 billion . . . . For 1979, the tax loss . . . would be over $50 billion."

Professor Gutmann went on to argue that reducing taxes would shift production and trade from the underground to the legal economy. Toward this end, the Reagan administration proposed a set of economic and fiscal changes that we will examine more closely in a later chapter. Whether people will report more of their income to the IRS with lower taxes, or whether they will continue to hide as much loot as they can from the scrutiny of Uncle Sam whatever the tax situation, will take a bit longer to find out.

Meanwhile, the revolution continues at a frenetic pace. In 1981, thirty-five hundred automobile workers in Flint, Michigan, joined together and claimed up to ninety-nine dependents on their withholding forms to give themselves automatic raises.

A California real estate magnate named Bill Greene wrote a book entitled *Win Your Personal Tax Revolt*, explaining how people could utilize paper losses to avoid paying income taxes. When the IRS summoned a grand jury to indict Greene for criminal tax evasion, the real-estate-man-turned-author put on a suit of armor and led a group of protesters on a march through San Francisco. His followers carried placards that read, "IRS! STAY OUT OF MY CHURCH!" "AUDIT THE IRS!" "NUKE THE IRS!" and similar sentiments.

"For years I have conducted my affairs in exactly the same way," said Greene, "having audits and settling my tax problems on a friendly basis. But as soon as I got a high profile, the IRS began what must have been a million-dollar investigation.

"These bastards have so much power they can take innocent citizens and screw them to the wall."

By the IRS's own admission, however, it is having a more difficult time processing the mountain of paperwork it is inundated with each year. In 1980 IRS was physically able to audit only 2.02 percent of total returns, a 5 percent decline from the year before. Former IRS agent Philip Storer admitted, "The agency is falling further and further behind in their audits. They don't have a large force, and they are in serious trouble."

Awareness of this has encouraged participants in the underground economy to be more brazen than ever before in their defiance of IRS. A growing number of American citizens are willing to take greater risks on the assumption that the IRS does not have the capacity to police the underground economy the way it would like to.

CHAPTER FOUR

The IRS Fights Back

The IRS Develops Its Strategy

Limited manpower or not, the IRS has announced plans to take up arms against the new American tax revolution that is sweeping the nation. In its annual report for the fiscal year ending September 30, 1980, the IRS admitted that it was physically able to audit only 2,179,297 returns out of the almost 91,000,000 that were filed the previous April. This was a significantly smaller percentage than the year before, and its auditing capacity was diminishing at a time when the underground economy was expanding at an alarming speed.

Despite its limited auditing ability, the IRS was able to collect $9.4 billion in additional taxes and penalties, a sharp improvement over the $7.1 billion it collected the year before. The message was clear: although the IRS is not able to scrutinize as many tax returns as it would like to, the ones it does go over will be raked with a fine-tooth comb. No more Mr. Nice Guy; the IRS is getting tough. By its own admission it has decided to use the "vinegar" approach. The "honey" approach—pleading with the public to voluntary comply with the tax code—simply doesn't work.

"I think it's obvious that they're auditing more efficiently," a tax accountant remarked prior to the April 15, 1981, filing date. "They're zeroing in on the big fish, using their computers more effectively."

Former IRS Commissioner Mortimer Caplin acknowledged that IRS is gearing up for a bare-knuckles brawl with the American public in the years ahead. "Collecting taxes from the underground economy may be the surest way to balance the budget," he said. "There's no question that you'll see a lot more vinegar used instead of honey in the future."

Caplin, who has apparently been recruited as the point man in the new get-tough policy, announced that the IRS is especially concerned about four broad categories of tax cheating. First, the revenue agents will be concentrating on the estimated 40 percent of income that is not reported by people with cash businesses. The agency is particularly interested in "sole proprietorships—Ma and Pa grocers, restaurant and movie theater operators, used-car dealers, . . . doctors and lawyers, and any other business that generates a lot of receipts in cash."

Second, the IRS wants to take a careful look at the "35 to 50 percent of all rental and royalty income which is not reported. Landlords, free-lance writers, oil well owners, and others are the villains here," said Caplin.

Third, tax collectors will be checking out the 17 to 22 percent of all capital gains on the sale of property that IRS estimates goes unreported. "This can include everyone from the high-rolling wheeler-dealer to the ordinary citizen who buys and sells a few shares of stock, or invests his nest egg in a duplex apartment," warned the former commissioner.

Finally, said Caplin, "Eight to 16 percent of interest and dividend income is unreported. This category potentially includes anybody with a savings account or corporate stock."

Among the remedies Caplin advocated to combat the tax rebellion are new personnel to examine more income tax returns in the future, an improvement in IRS capacity to match the data it receives with individual tax returns, and tax withholding at the source on all dividend and interest payments.

"There is nothing wrong in having your tax return checked for accuracy," said Caplin. "We all do it with grocery bills and bank statements. Why shouldn't the government do it for tax bills?"

At present, the IRS has fewer than 20,000 revenue agents to monitor an anticipated 140 million returns of all types that will come flooding into its offices in 1982 from every corner of the nation. By Caplin's own admission, this is not nearly enough to handle all the returns the agency would like to audit. "The long odds against being audited make outright tax cheaters give themselves the benefit of every conceivable doubt." Caplin wants the Reagan administration to hire thousands of new examiners who are especially trained as sophisticated tax auditors.

He also wants IRS computers upgraded to digest the mind-numbing total of 500 million separate pieces of data the agency is bombarded with each year. Half of this material now comes in on magnetic tape, and the IRS is getting better at matching this electronic information against individual tax returns. For instance, a good deal of dividend and interest payment data is put on magnetic tape and fed to the IRS by banks and brokerage firms. This is easier for the tax agency to program into its computers and compare against the social security numbers on tax returns to check them for accuracy. However, the other quarter of a billion pieces of information—royalty payments, rental income, fees paid to independent contractors, some salary figures—are received on paper, amounting to an unmanageable avalanche of documents that the IRS is incapable of processing. As much as 70 percent of this paper data is fed into shredding machines and destroyed before the agency even glances at it. In the years ahead, IRS will be lobbying to get all these facts and figures on magnetic tape so they can be stored in its computers for future reference.

Caplin's last proposal, one he has been advocating for a decade or longer, is for taxes on interest and dividend payments to be withheld at the source in the same fashion as withholding taxes on salary checks. Government figures indicate that it would collect an additional $3 to 4 billion alone through this measure.

"It seems foolhardy to pass up such an opportunity," said Caplin.

In addition to Caplin's remedies, the IRS will also be changing the way it selects tax returns for audit. Since 1955, income tax returns have been classified according to adjusted gross income, or AGI. AGI is your total income minus all the deductions you take; in other words, the amount of income you actually pay taxes on. Shrewd individuals with high incomes are able to arrive at a low AGI through the use of tax shelters, business expenses, depreciation, and other sophisticated write-offs. Until now, AGI was the only figure IRS looked at when picking returns for audit, which meant that a lot of taxpayers with huge tax-sheltered income (precisely those IRS wanted to be auditing in the first place) escaped careful scrutiny.

Slowly, like an overstuffed dinosaur gearing up for a change in direction, IRS has been revamping its system to check tax returns according to TPI, or total positive income, instead of AGI. TPI means exactly that—everything you declare as income before the shelters and deductions come into play. This way, the reasoning goes, the agency will be able to get a closer look at people with really big incomes. It all sounds so simple, one wonders why the dinosaur never thought of it before.

Included in TPI is something the IRS refers to, in typical bureaucratic fashion, as TGR, which stands for total gross receipts. TGR, you ought to know, includes the sum of all receipts from business income that is reported on Schedule C and farm income, Schedule F, as well as the amount you earn as salary. The IRS's alphabet-soup method of conducting business is undergoing a fundamental change that could significantly improve the quality of its audits, even as the quantity continues to decline.

"No matter how carefully a taxpayer prepares his or her return item by item, the IRS is concerned now more than ever about the amount of income that the taxpayer has before subtracting any deductions or losses," said George Jones, a tax attorney for the legal publishing firm of Matthew Bender & Co., during the 1981 tax season.

Other improvements IRS has declared it will be marking in its ongoing battle against the underground economy include a hard line against foreign or offshore tax havens and other intricate shelters, in an effort to tighten the loopholes for the wealthy; an investigation into the barter industry, and close scrutiny of barter clubs and trade exchanges, to make sure taxpayers report "income" received in cash-free transactions; enforcement of legal and ethical standards of accountants, lawyers, and other tax advisers who dream up sophisticated shelters and deductions for their wealthy clients; a crackdown on mail-order pastors, Fifth Amendment protesters, and visible tax rebels like Irwin Schiff who flaunt their defiance of the IRS in the media; and a war against known drug dealers, pimps and prostitutes, and racketeers who operate on the far side of the law.

Last but not least, the IRS is officially on record now as favoring a "simplified tax code" to make compliance easier and more palatable for the honest American citizen. Amazing! It took a $700 billion underground economy to make the dinosaur start thinking about a simplified system of taxation that might have defused the revolution before it ever got started.

The Great Computer Network— Where Your Return Goes

Under the current system, what happens to your tax return after you pop it in the mail to IRS resembles a cartoon series of events straight from the brain of Rube Goldberg.

The IRS maintains ten regional centers, staffed with thirty-five thousand employees who waded through more than 100 million tax returns in 1981. Incoming envelopes are slit open by machines at a speed of thirty thousand an hour. The coded IRS envelopes that are provided in the forms you receive in the mail are sorted automatically, while handwritten and other noncoded envelopes are processed by hand. The slit envelopes are passed along to clerks at "tingle tables," who then separate the returns into groups—those with checks for tax payments and those without checks requesting a refund. Complicated returns are rerouted to experienced clerks, who sort them out for closer examination later.

The returns with obvious mistakes, such as missing signatures or missing W-2 forms and other documents, are returned immediately to the taxpayers. Returns with mistakes of different kinds, such as poor addition or unallowable deductions, are set aside and flagged for special processing. Letters requesting explanations for these errors start going out in July; more than half a million were sent out in 1981, and the number increases every year, in proportion to the complexity of the tax laws and forms we have to fill out.

After your return passes through this initial screening process, it is stamped with an identification number and fed into a computer, which checks it in greater detail for accuracy. If the computer finds a mistake in arithmetic or calculation, corrections are made whether they favor you or the IRS. More than 7 percent of total returns had mistakes in calculation in 1981, and this percentage, too, is increasing each year. A special team of investigators then checks all the data for phony returns. Nearly five thousand fakes were uncovered in 1981, filed by schemers who falsified W-2 statements and used fictitious names and social security numbers in order to get refunds they weren't entitled to. In one case, examiners discovered an otherwise respectable executive who had collected over $400,000 illegally from the IRS.

Having gotten this far through the regional center's computer, that innocent return you sent in is now forwarded to the main IRS computer center in Martinsburg, West Virginia, where it is either selected for audit or cleared for a refund. A full 80 percent of all returns qualify for refunds each year, and the average refund check for individuals was close to $700 in 1981. By June 1982, IRS estimates that over 80 million refund checks will have been mailed out from six regional disbursing offices of the Treasury Department.

Your refund check, however, should you be fortunate enough to receive one, is no guarantee that that is the last you will be hearing from the IRS this year. Your return is stored on a master tape for five years, while microfilm records are kept for decades. The actual paper return itself is eventually buried in a federal warehouse, but record on magnetic tape occupies only two-tenths of an inch at the main computer center. As additional data is received concerning wages and income, dividend and interest payments, royalty earnings and other pertinent information, it is continally matched against the social security number on your master file. Should a discrepancy ever arise between the figures you reported and the ones the IRS receives on magnetic tape, you could be called in for an audit. At present, the IRS has a secret formula for selecting certain returns for special audit, but various taxpayer groups are suing under the Freedom of Information Act to make it public. The IRS is resisting, maintaining that publicizing this formula would eliminate one of its primary means of keeping people honest.

An IRS audit, contrary to what the nightmares of most taxpayers would indicate, does not necessarily end in disaster for the individual. Last year, 69 percent of the audits resulted in additional taxes and penalties averaging $1,563. Twenty-four percent of the audited returns were left unchanged, while IRS had to return an average of $2,900 to the final 7 percent.

When you consider how much time, labor, and money is wasted by government in collecting revenues from its otherwise loyal citizens, one recurring thought comes immediately to mind: surely there must be an easier way.

The Crackdown on the Individual Taxpayer—A Move Away from the Organized Crime Patrol

In an interview conducted during the tax season last year, IRS Commissioner Roscoe L. Egger, Jr., said that, until that "easier way" was found, the IRS's vinegar approach to collecting money for the government would remain in force. He intended to take a hard line toward tax cheaters in several key areas.

"We've taken immediate steps in those areas where we find that illegal tax protesters have persuaded people in significant numbers to file erroneous or illegal W-4 withholding forms," Egger said. He was referring specifically to the auto workers who were claiming ninety-nine dependents on their W-4 forms to eliminate withholding tax. Employers throughout the country were notified early in 1981 to question any employees who seemed to be claiming dependents far above the number they were entitled to. The IRS reserved the right to lower this figure arbitrarily unless the individual taxpayer could show that he or she had enough deductions to justify the claim.

As far as the visible leaders of the tax rebellion are concerned, "We are going after them," said Egger. "Some are already under indictment or behind bars. We don't intend to stop or slow down in the vigor with which we pursue these people."

Besides pursuing the self-styled revolutionaries and rebels, Egger was also worried about the problem of noncompliance among self-employed people. "Pretty clearly, the problem of underreporting of income is especially troublesome among self-employed persons," he added. This problem he intended to deal with through the IRS's new, upgraded audit-selection process. "Our taxpayer-compliance measurement program, which makes special in-depth audits, attempts to get the statistical data we need to help us select on a more accurate basis which returns to examine."

In other words, if you work in certain sensitive areas by IRS standards, you are presumed guilty until proven innocent, and you stand a greater chance of being audited than anyone else.

Part of this process involves "the ability to put better information in the hands of examining revenue agents with regard to income on which tax hasn't been withheld. In the past, an agent might have had to research that himself. Now when an agent begins an examination, the file includes the information returns on that type of income."

In plain English, the examining IRS agent will be comparing the amount of your specific deductions with the averages for your "type," and you will be called upon to prove any deductions you take that exceed these averages.

Tax shelters are another prime source of irritation to Mr. Egger. "The IRS has a special program to deal with returns that include tax shelters. Right now, we have about two hundred thousand cases under active examination. So we're pursuing it vigorously.

"The shelters that we're concerned about are the ones that do not appear to have any economic purpose other than to avoid or defer taxes. The commodity straddle," Egger specified, "in which gains made in futures trading are pushed into later years for tax purposes, is a classic case of that. Some of these abusive shelters will be attacked in the courts, some legislatively."

IRS wants Congress to enact a law making it possible to tax certain fringe benefits and other "perks" enjoyed by businessmen. In many cases, an executive will opt for a perk rather than a salary increase to avoid paying extra taxes. "Such things," said Egger, "as free travel for airplane employees and free tuition for children of college professors" as well as expense accounts and stock options should be considered income and taxed accordingly.

However, Egger was not as optimistic as Mortimer Caplin was about the prospect of a withholding tax on dividend and interest income. "Tax enforcement is easier if you have withholding because collection is automatic. But, being politically realistic, I suspect greater withholding is not going to happen," he admitted.

What about public resistance to any tough new measures taken by the IRS? What would happen if millions of people got sore and refused to report their incomes voluntarily?

"If taxpayers in those numbers refused, the system simply wouldn't work," Egger answered, giving voice to the same fear expressed by former IRS Commissioner Donald Alexander in the early 1970s when he admitted that the one thing government feared more than anything else was a well-organized middle-class tax rebellion.

"But I don't see that happening," Egger added quickly.

Is there any danger of the IRS overstepping its authority in its campaign against the taxpaying public and engaging in what some people might regard as gestapo tactics?

"There have been some misunderstandings," explained Egger. "I want to dispel fear of the IRS, to get the public to understand that, merely because they get a letter from us, this doesn't mean they should start to shake. They should be able to assume that it's a friendly letter unless their conscience tells them otherwise."

Despite these reassurances from Egger, evidence is already growing that the IRS is far more concerned about collecting money from the citizenry any way it can than it is about polishing its public relations image. Starting in 1979, the IRS began engaging in tactics that indicated it was acting as a law unto itself without regard for taxpayers' rights or interests. Some IRS critics have claimed that, since the agency is virtually impotent in its war against organized crime and other high-powered elements of society, it is taking out its wrath on the ordinary citizen who has neither the influence nor the wherewithal to defend himself properly.

A businessman in Portland, Maine, was the victim of an embezzlement that created a $20,000 tax delinquency in his business. He worked out what he thought was a deal with the IRS to pay off his debt at a rate of $2,000 a month, and these payments were kept up faithfully for several months when, without warning, IRS swooped down like a vulture and simply extracted $9,000 from his bank account to clear up the balance.

At that, he was far better off than the owner of a small business in Michigan, who found himself in arrears to the IRS for the tidy sum of $40,000. Like the Maine businessman, the small business owner in Michigan had been victimized by an embezzler and did not deliberately try to defraud the government. In retaliation, IRS went to court and imposed a $400,000 lien on his property, ten times what he owed, to satisfy his debt. He paid off $20,000 of his obligation with cash he was able to scrape together, then covered the balance shortly afterward. Apparently to teach him a lesson he would never forget, IRS took its own sweet time releasing the lien, tying up his assets and his ability to conduct business and make a living for months after the delinquent taxes were paid.

Incredible as it sounds, living in a "free and open society" as we repeatedly boast, the IRS's actions in both situations were absolutely legal under its own regulations and the authority granted to the agency by our representatives in Congress. According to columnist Jack Anderson, who might have seemed guilty of overstatement just a short while ago, "IRS officials have become the rulers of the American public they are supposed to serve."

Susan Long, a Princeton Visiting Fellow specializing in IRS training techniques, claimed that this "them-against-us" mentality is ingrained in all IRS employees from the time they are hired. "They are taught," said Long, "that most people cheat and you're hated, and that puts them on the defensive right from the start."

A major problem with the way IRS operates, said Long, is the fact that each local office is run like a personal fiefdom, subject to the whim of the district supervisor. While seizures of personal property are supposed to be a "last resort against hard-core tax evaders," in reality IRS officials have a great deal of leeway and can order them virtually at their own discretion. Robert Starkey, who took over as head of the IRS Collection Division in 1979, certainly hasn't discouraged the practice, although he maintained that he did not set quotas for his agents and that excessive property seizures are "wrong and not national policy."

Still, under his reign, these seizures increased dramatically, going from 5,723 to 9,423 in the space of a single year.

Perhaps taking his lead from his boss Robert Starkey, a supervisor in Saint Louis sent a memo to his subordinates in 1979 which, according to columnist Jack Anderson, asked rhetorically, "Why aren't your revenue officers making seizures? It is painfully apparent that other districts are getting more out of their revenue officers in terms of using this enforcement tool."

His memo, which sounded more like a threat than anything else, did not go unheeded. A year later, the supervisor gloated, property seizures in his district more than doubled.

The same is true of other districts throughout the United States. Everywhere you look, the pattern is the same. On August 2, 1979, Mr. and Mrs. Stephen Oliver locked themselves inside their 1970 Volkswagen in front of their house in Fairbanks, Alaska. Surrounding them were half a dozen IRS special agents, armed with nightsticks and pistols, demanding that they surrender their car as partial payment of $3,300 the Olivers owed in back taxes. When the Olivers refused to unlock the doors, the team of agents proceeded to smash in the windows with their nightsticks and drag the terrified couple (now the former owners of the Volkswagen) bodily from the car. IRS was simply exercising its legal "power of distraint and seizure by any means," which gives the agency the right to seize personal property at its own discretion when it ascertains that taxes are due.

The Olivers were victims of the IRS's new policy of harassing ordinary taxpayers while leaving mobsters and other underworld figures alone. Off the record, agents admit that the ordinary citizen is less likely to burn down an agent's house or rub out members of his family for seizing his property than a drug dealer is. It's strictly a matter of common sense; pick on the guy who is less likely to fight back and inflict bodily harm on the tax collector. In Miami, the clearing center for much of the $40 billion annual drug business in the United States, Cuban racketeers openly threatened the lives of agents who came snooping into their neighborhoods and have been left alone as a result. The same is true of drug peddlers in San Francisco, New York City, Atlantic City, and other cities where big-time hoods and their highly paid lawyers and accountants rake in money hand-over-fist in defiance of the law. The IRS is pursuing the nickle-and-dime tax evader, where the pickings are easier, and staying out of the danger zones.

In Idaho, IRS agents put padlocks on small business establishments that were a few thousand dollars behind in tax payments and chained the cars of individual citizens to utility poles until their taxes were paid. In Las Vegas, 170 full-time agents were assigned to spy on the casinos—not on the owners of the casinos which do hundreds of millions of dollars each year in cash receipts, but on the busboys, waitresses, chambermaids, and croupiers whom the IRS suspected of pocketing tips without reporting them on their returns. When Senator Paul Laxalt of Nevada, who is now a top aide to Ronald Reagan, learned of this operation, he exploded in rage on the floor of the Senate. "The high-handed bureaucratic excesses of the IRS are a national disgrace. Evidence reveals that the IRS singles out areas of the country for special enforcement. It will go completely against congressional intent and thirty years of past policy by changing its rules to squeeze out more revenue. We appear to be witnessing an agency totally out of control, running roughshod over taxpayers and making a joke out of our rule of laws. The cases of abuse are easy to document and too numerous to count."

Off the record, IRS agents concede that much of what Senator Laxalt charges is true, but they are only following orders passed down from higher levels of command. The individual agent in the field has been specifically ordered to stay away from the big-time criminal cases and go after the "penny cases" involving middle-class taxpayers who are unable to fight back and pay up quietly and quickly when IRS goes after them.

"Right now," said Robert Rust, a former federal attorney who specialized in tax cases a few years back, "the IRS is harassing the middle-class businessman and the mom-and-pop grocery stores. It is not putting forth the major effort it should with regard to those individuals involved in the trafficking of money and narcotics, cases which other police agencies have great difficulty in making. The IRS is involved in rinky-dink cases."

"They've shot all the tigers and put the rabbits in charge," Richard Jaffe, a former IRS field supervisor for the Criminal Investigation Division, agreed. "It's a joke. Talk to any IRS man any place in the country, and they'll all tell you the same thing: we've been told to stay away from the big organized-crime and drug cases. We're told to make the little cases . . . the traditional small-time cheaters like small businessmen, doctors, and others in the middle class."

Is fear for their lives the only reason the IRS has abandoned its traditional war on racketeers such as Al Capone and Frank Costello?

That's only part of it, answered an IRS special agent who chose to remain anonymous. The most important reasons are more complicated than that.

"First, major tax cases are very difficult to make; they take a long time and are extremely difficult to prosecute. Figure that to prosecute a major tax-evasion case will cost about fifty thousand dollars." In a nutshell, it makes more sense for IRS to scare up small amounts of money from many different taxpayers than to try for a big score against a few powerful individuals who can drag their cases out for years.

"Second . . . most of your major tax violators are politically well-connected. . . . The big thing today is drugs. I've seen big, legitimate businesses which were actually founded by money earned from cocaine smuggling—millions of dollars. That's hard to fight, especially when all that money is spread around in political contributions. Let's face it: these days money spent in the right circles will buy you immunity from tax prosecutions; there's no doubt about it."

Ironically enough, much of the power the IRS enjoys today in its persecution of average, middle-class taxpayers was derived from the days when it was stepping up its campaign against racketeers such as Al Capone. Later, in the early 1950s, the IRS was limited in its ability to investigate big-name underworld figures effectively. As a result, it was given the authority to create an intelligence division (IRSID) specifically to coordinate tax cases against major criminals who had escaped prosecution on other charges. The idea was, if the government couldn't nail them for anything else, why not get them for tax evasion?

IRSID, in its officially sanctioned crusade against the Mafia, ran havoc over the libertarian rights guaranteed in the U.S. Constitution. Wiretaps were used without court orders, illegal searches and seizures conducted without concern about the Fourth Amendment, and other racketeers were blackmailed and bribed into turning witness against their underworld confederates. No one cared much, since these were "only mobsters" IRS was pursuing and, in the days before *The Godfather* at least, the Mafia was considered to be alien and un-American.

Now, of course, all the dons and their various buttonmen and capos have been turned into All-American folk heroes. Wonders never cease.

IRSID did its appointed job so effectively that further uses for its service were concocted by a string of presidents starting with John F. Kennedy and ending with Richard Nixon. Kennedy gave IRSID the authority to form something called the Ideological Organizations Project to exert tax pressure against certain right-wing groups such as the John Birch Society and Facts Forum, H. L. Hunt's rather exotic propaganda machine, which had been conducting virulent smear campaigns against the Kennedy administration; Lyndon Johnson used IRSID as a personal secret police force of sorts to make sure that certain congressmen voted the way he wanted them to on key programs; and Richard Nixon enlisted the services of IRSID to audit and harass his multitude of "enemies," imagined or otherwise. It wasn't until Nixon's departure that the new (in 1973) IRS Commissioner, Donald Alexander, acted to dismantle much of IRSID's extraconstitutional powers and change its name to the Criminal Investigation Division, all in the spirit of the post-Watergate purges that were taking place.

But critics of the IRS assert that most of Alexander's reforms were organizational and were never really enacted into law. As a result, the renamed intelligence unit still retains on paper most of the powers it was granted in the early 1950s. Whether it makes use of them is strictly dependent on the whim of whoever happens to be in charge at any particular moment.

And so it has come to pass that the Criminal Investigation Division of the IRS, which was originally created as an intelligence unit to combat organized crime, has unleashed its awesome power against ordinary citizens while hardened criminals pretty much go their own way.

Keeping the Taxpayer in Line—A Perpetual State of Anxiety

Meanwhile, the IRS vinegar campaign against the American taxpayer continues to gain momentum. In 1981 the agency inaugurated an eight-year, $218 million program to upgrade its equipment so that it can match income data against individual returns more effectively. It also plans to work more closely with the Social Security Administration to get additional data on individuals, including current addresses when they move, stored in its computers. Within the next few years the IRS hopes to completely overhaul its master-file, management, scheduling, and processing systems to shorten the time it takes to match data against returns; in 1981 it took the IRS three years to process one year's data completely; by the late 1980s the IRS hopes to reduce this to a matter of months.

In the months and years ahead, IRS will also be digging deeper to uncover income that has been difficult to trace so far. It will be using a system known as "total positive worth," taking into consideration an individual's whole visible lifestyle in determining taxable income. IRS agents will be trying to find out what kind of car you drive, how much cash you have in your checking and savings accounts, what kind of investment portfolio you have, the market value of your house, what kind of assets you purchased recently, how much money you spend on vacations and entertainment—in short, your entire standard of living—in an effort to determine how much you should be earning to afford it all. So, for example, someone living in a $200,000 house, with two Mercedes-Benzes sitting in the driveway, who took his family on a three-week vacation to Europe within the past twelve months, and reported $15,000 in annual income to IRS, could suddenly find an IRS agent ascertaining that, in reality, he must have earned at least $100,000 last year to maintain such a high standard of living.

Any taxpayer whom IRS determines to have understated more than $10,000 in income for the year will be referred to the Criminal Investigation Division for closer examination.

In related instances, IRS also challenged more than eight hundred people in the New York metropolitan area who listed themselves as ministers last year, claiming 100 percent tax exemptions, and over five thousand other mail-order ministers scattered throughout the country.

"People who make bona fide gifts to churches give a low percentage of their incomes and get no benefits in return," explained Joseph Jelonek, an IRS agent especially assigned to these cases. The IRS, he added, is now going after people "whose gifts are 50 percent to 100 percent of their incomes."

Starting in 1980, anyone called in for an IRS audit, found himself or herself asked at the start of the interview, "Are you a member of a barter or trade club, and did you receive any goods or services in trade?"

This is part of the IRS's growing concern about the mushrooming barter industry in the United States and its attempt to tax a piece of the action.

"We tell our members constantly, 'For God's sake,

pay your taxes. This is all extra business we're providing you with, so why not pay your taxes on it?' Of course, whether they do or not is strictly up to them. We can't make out their returns for them," said a principal of Barter Systems of Southern Connecticut in May 1981.

"Has IRS made any determination about the value of a trade unit?" I asked.

"We have a working understanding with IRS that they'll settle for fifty cents on the dollar. In other words, a member who did 10,000 trade units worth of business with us last year is supposed to claim an additional $5,000 in income."

"Are they making you turn over your records to help them enforce compliance?"

"Not yet, and we'll resist doing that as long as we can. Right now it's still up to each individual. But even with this fifty-cents-on-the-dollar ruling, a lot of members still squawk. They want us to take the position that all this barter business is nothing more than a bookkeeping procedure—rearranging of inventory and so on. How it'll all work out a few years from now is anyone's guess."

It will probably take a federal court decision to ascertain whether bartering, indeed, is nothing more than "rearrangement of inventory" and bookkeeping procedure, or whether it results in an actual increase in material worth that should be taxed at fair market value. Until this decision is made, however, the IRS's *Audit Technique Handbook* will continue to instruct revenue agents "to be alert to the possibility of bartering or swapping techniques or schemes when verifying income."

The IRS will also be taking a harder look at non-cash donations to charity, particularly when the amount exceeds $5,000, to see if taxpayers are inflating the fair market value of their gifts. In 1981 the agency came up with a formula designed to tell auditing agents at precisely what income levels these abuses are most likely to occur. If circumstances warrant, said an IRS spokesman, certain "types" of returns will automatically be selected for audit, with special attention given to deductions for gifts of gemstones, books, stamps, and similar items. In April 1981, the IRS decided to select about ten thousand 1979 returns for special review in this particular area to see if any "abusive pattern emerged."

The IRS, apparently, intends to keep the American taxpayer in a perpetual state of anxiety by saying, in effect, that the door is never closed on your return for any year. It can be reopened any time the IRS decides to go back and have a look for any reason it wants to.

Yes, the battle lines are clearly drawn. The American taxpayer is more indignant than ever about rising taxes, horrendous inflation, which is the most insidious tax of all, and governmental abuses; the IRS, in a massive effort to crack down on tax evasion and break the back of the underground economy, is violating the constitutional rights of the citizenry more and more.

Moreover, the fine line between illegal tax protesters and ordinary citizens who hide some of their income or cheat a bit on their returns does not even exist any more. As far as the IRS is concerned, it's an "us-against-them" revolution, with all American taxpayers cast by the agency in the role of the "enemy." The IRS has lumped all taxpayers together as adversaries, and it is not too concerned about the particular degree of protest.

Nonfilers and stop-filers; Fifth Amendment protesters; mail-order ministers; owners of mom-and-pop stores and other cash businesses; members of barter clubs; businessmen who utilize tax shelters to reduce the tax burden; dentists, doctors, and accountants; waitresses, taxi drivers, chambermaids, and others who work for tips; everyone, in short, who earns reportable income is a potential enemy as far as the IRS is concerned. By making an example of some of the more brazen violators of the U.S. tax code, IRS hopes to make honest citizens of the rest.

Will the IRS Meet Its Goals?

Whether IRS can do all it says it will do, however, is open to question. According to several former revenue agents who, like former CIA operatives, have grown disenchanted and written exposés about their ex-employers, IRS is not nearly as omnipotent as it would have us believe.

"Nothing is more important to the IRS strategy than scaring the taxpayer, and keeping it that way," said Paul Strassels after the publication of his book, *All You Need to Know About the IRS*. "Each year they issue a package of news stories about people who have gone to prison for tax fraud just to get you thinking about it. And when they audit someone they hope the word will get around about what an awful experience it is.

"First of all," Strassels continued, "the IRS computers are not all they're cracked up to be. In 1976, the IRS asked for super computers and the federal Office of Management and Budget wouldn't approve it because it didn't want such a high-powered collection system operating in the United States. The IRS would like you to think it's high-powered, but you can blow the whole system by simply listing the wife's name and Social Security number first on a joint return. They won't be able to match any records because the computer is programed to read the husband first."

Barry Steiner, another former IRS auditor, corroborated Strassels's statements. "If taxpayers understood that IRS agents are only human, the whole image would be blown. The system wouldn't work."

Steiner claimed that he was under constant pressure to carry his share, which meant bringing in a certain amount of money each day from his audits.

"During one of my first audits I ended up giving back some money, and I got called in by my supervisor who wanted to know what was going on. After that I learned the unwritten rule—if you bring in $100 of extra tax money every hour, you are just earning your keep. How much more you bring in determines how fast you are promoted."

Strassels, Steiner, and two other ex-IRS agents, Mary Sprouse and Edward Vitkus, agreed that taxpayers could reduce their risk of being audited by following a few tested rules: first of all, if you are a tax protester, don't advertise this fact on your return. Anyone using the Fifth Amendment or similar reasons for not completing their tax returns will automatically be audited. Second, file as close to the April 15 deadline as possible, since your return will be "less visible" then than it is in February and March when a lot of short forms are filed and returns are generally scattered. Third, if you have a lot of deductions, learn which ones are "safe" and which will invite closer scrutiny. For example, interest payments on mortgages, credit cards, and installment debt are rarely questioned since they are so easily verified. The same is true of cash payments to charity, state income tax and sales and property taxes, casualty losses, union and professional organization dues, dependents, capital gains and losses if they are not too complicated, tax preparation fees, and charges for safe deposit boxes (although you might think twice about claiming this since the IRS can get into your safe deposit box as easily as it can slap a lien on your bank account if you owe any back taxes).

On the other hand, you are treading on thin ice once you start claiming some of the more "abusive" tax shelters, an office in your home, high travel and entertainment expenses, interest-free loans to children, and business expenses for a family operation. You should also be aware that if you are a doctor, dentist, airline pilot, celebrity, or a self-employed entrepreneur, you are working in one of the "sensitive areas" the IRS has designated for special treatment.

Finally, the individual you select to prepare your tax return can also be significant, since the IRS maintains a "hit list" of tax preparers whom it considers to be indulging more in fiction than in fact as far as tax write-offs are concerned.

One final caveat from the former auditors: the rules can change at any moment and most likely will. The IRS is building up momentum as it plans its strategy for the struggle ahead. Everything is in a state of flux, and it behooves the taxpayer to be constantly on the alert. The price of liberty, said Thomas Jefferson, another rebel from a different era, is eternal vigilance.

The battle promises to be a momentous one, since, as the IRS develops its own get-tough strategy, leaders of the various tax-protest groups throughout the country are planning counterattacks of their own.

"This tax revolt is so far gone there is no way the IRS can keep up with it. Now that this thing is out in the open, it's going like wildfire," said Ed Marshall, the forty-seven-year-old leader of We the People ACT (American Citizens Tribunal), the group that organized the withholding rebellion among thirty-five hundred automobile workers in Michigan in the spring of 1981. Marshall, who is a truck driver himself, maintained that, despite IRS claims that the rebellion was under control, in reality it was spreading from Flint to Pontiac and Detroit, with new members joining all the time.

On another battle front, the Church of Scientology, a well-financed international organization, stepped up efforts on behalf of Fifth Amendment protesters in May 1981. Tim Skog, a church leader, said that the IRS was not telling the American public the whole truth regarding the legal standing of Fifth Amendment protesters. The IRS's *Illegal Tax Protester Training* manual, first published in 1979, states candidly that there is a rapidly increasing number of protesters who are "attempting to disrupt effective tax administration and present a major danger to our voluntary compliance system." The manual maintains that a 1927 Supreme Court decision, *United States* v. *Sullivan*, denies the taxpayer the right to "refuse to file a federal income tax return based on the Fifth Amendment right against self-incrimination."

What this IRS manual carefully neglects to mention, said Skog, is that a 1976 Supreme Court case, *Garner* v. *United States*, determined that "the Fifth Amendment right can be claimed on a tax return," and the legal aspects of this situation are still being contested. IRS is acting as though this form of protest is illegal, said Skog, but the courts have not had the final word yet. The Church of Scientology is just one of many litigants challenging the IRS on this particular issue, while a laundry list of other grievances will be fought in the courts for years to come.

On a different level, more orthodox antitax organizations such as the National Taxpayers Union and the National Tax Limitation Committee announced plans to step up their lobbying efforts in Washington, D.C., for sharp reductions in federal taxes. The movement to cut back both on taxes and federal expenditures through the legal system will be escalating in coming years. Many proponents of lower taxes and a smaller role for government in the affairs of the nation expect that their programs, once implemented, will go a long way toward bringing most of that hidden income out there to the surface, thereby dismantling the underground economy before it reaches the trillion dollar mark.

Will lower taxes induce the American people to declare all their income and pay their taxes honestly? Or is it human nature to hang on to as much money as we can, all of it if possible, no matter how equitable the tax system? A lot of what happens during the next few years depends a great deal on the programs set in motion by the administration in the nation's capital. The message coming out of Washington, during the early stages of the Reagan presidency at least, is nothing less than revolutionary. Whether the reality coincides with the fiery rhetoric will become clearer as time passes.

Let's take a look now at this would-be revolution in progress, and the impact it is likely to have on the underground economy.

—————— CHAPTER FIVE ——————

The Rebellion Continues

Enter the Reagan Revolution

There is no question that the Reagan administration, with its program of tax cuts and investment incentives for individuals and businesses, would like to turn us all into honest, law-abiding citizens. The IRS budget has not been spared by Reagan's budget-cutting aides, and various spokesmen for the administration adopted an anti-IRS, protaxpayer stance shortly after President Reagan took his oath of office.

"I don't think that an army of IRS agents swarming throughout the country is the best way to win the support of the American people for the government in Washington," Secretary of the Treasury Donald Regan remarked to an audience of appreciative businessmen in April 1981.

To drive this message home with even greater force, President Reagan announced shortly after Regan's speech that the IRS bureaucracy would be trimmed along with everyone else's. While the IRS was lobbying hard for more money to upgrade its computer-surveillance system, the president ordered the agency to reduce its staff by six thousand employees, which, he said, would result in a saving of $146 million a year. The IRS complained loudly, stating that such a personnel cutback would lose the government over a billion dollars a year in uncollected taxes. Former President Jimmy Carter had planned to increase IRS personnel in fiscal year 1982, had he been reelected, and raise the agency's budget as well. But Reagan was unmoved. Fewer people, said he, would be motivated to cheat on their taxes once his tax cuts were passed. Therefore, fewer auditors would be needed.

Whether this is wishful thinking remains to be seen. There is no question that the IRS's ability to pursue its war on the underground economy will be directly tied to the personnel and funding it has at its disposal. This less-than-hospitable mood toward the IRS in the nation's capital, emanating from the president himself, has got to hurt it somewhat. The diligence with which the agency sets about its task of squeezing funds out of a reluctant citizenry will likewise be determined to a great extent by the mood of the nation's leader.

"In the view of most of Reagan's economists," wrote Ernest Volkman and John Cummings in the April 1981 issue of *Penthouse*, "[tax] reductions will also end the so-called Underground Economy, the proliferating system under which many taxpayers simply overlook paying taxes on their income as a means of quiet protest against the system. That economy . . . will be reduced, the economists argue, by merely reducing the tax rates that force middle-class taxpayers into such a sub-rosa system."

Others outside the administration, however, are not so sure. A lot depends on how successful the president is in achieving his stated goal of balancing the federal budget by fiscal 1984. If federal revenues fall off substantially as a result of his own tax-reduction measures, and the budget remains hopelessly out of balance, Reagan might be sorely tempted to raise taxes once again and go after some of that unreported underground loot with a vengeance. In other words, the success or failure of Reagan's own economic program will determine the size of the underground economy a few years from now. We can all speculate as to just how successful the Reagan administration's economic policy is going to be, but only the passage of time will provide us with a definitive answer.

A Worldwide Phenomenon—Italy, France, West Germany, Great Britain, and Sweden (to Name a Few)

As enormous as the underground economy is in the United States, it is still considerably smaller (in proportion to total economic activity) than it is throughout most of western Europe. Several studies have placed underground business activity in the United States at slightly less than 10 percent of all recorded economic activity. In Italy the underground economy is estimated to be a staggering 35 percent of the aboveground economy, while the French version amounted to some 25 percent of the legal economy prior to the election of François Mitterand. It is expected to grow even larger as Mitterand's socialist policies take hold. Similarly, West Germany, Great Britain, and even formerly docile Sweden are estimated to have larger proportionate underground economies than does the United States.

What all these countries have in common is a larger tax burden than the United States. While this does not represent a scientific survey, there does not seem to be much doubt that painfully high taxes have resulted in fairly brisk underground economies throughout the world. In countries where taxes are higher than they are in the United States, the underground economies are proportionately larger. *Travail au noir* in France, *lavoro nero* in Italy, *schwarzarbeiter* in Germany, and *fiddling* in Great Britain all translate into the same principle: tax the citizenry at too high a rate, and they will hide their income from work performed off the books.

At this writing, President Reagan is the only leader of a major country who has tried the novel approach of reducing taxes as a means of eliminating the underground economy and expanding the above-ground, private economy. Margaret Thatcher of Great Britain talked a good deal about reducing the tax burden on English citizens when she assumed office, but, during the past few years, her combination of tax cuts in some areas and increases in others has resulted in a net tax increase for the English taxpayer. In France, Mitterand came to office with a highly publicized program of nationalizing a good deal of the economy and raising taxes.

"Mitterand's socialists may believe they can boost taxes, and yet, through bureaucratic policing, prevent widespread evasion," said a French economist who chose not to be identified, shortly after the Socialist victory, "but that won't work. Frenchmen have too much imagination. What has been a tendency of many French people now will develop into a stampede."

During the next few years we will have the opportunity to see whether the Reagan philosophy is working as far as the underground economy is concerned. Reagan and his advisers believe that people need incentives to participate fully and productively in the above-ground economy. Without the necessary incentives, they will drop out and cheat on their taxes; they will borrow and consume rather than save; they will shift capital into nonproductive areas; they will look for off-the-books income to avoid taxes; and they will pursue leisure rather than work.

The greatest incentive for people to work honestly and pay their taxes, according to the Reagan philosophy, is to allow them to enjoy the fruits of their labor, to enable them to see a real improvement in their standard of living, and to have the freedom to invest their money productively without having profits taxed away to such a point that it falls behind the rate of inflation. If people fail to make a *real* return on their investments, they will spend their earnings rather than save and invest for the future.

A Look at the Reagan Tax Cuts—Making Capitalism Respectable

To bolster their philosophical arguments with some measure of evidence, the Reagan economists like to cite various facts and figures. They argue that the underground economy tripled as a percentage of gross national product during the 1970s, a time when taxes were rising and inflation soared into the stratosphere.

Conversely, during the 1920s, when then-Secretary of the Treasury Andrew Mellon sharply reduced taxes that had been imposed during World War I, real GNP in the United States rose 54 percent and output per man-hour rose 66.5 percent. In other words, lower taxes, in this particular instance at least, resulted in a more dynamic private economy with more people participating productively in it. No one bothered to measure underground economic activity at the time, since it was not perceived as a problem, so we have no way of knowing if lower taxes succeeded in diminishing the size of the underground economy as well. But it is a reasonable assumption that a burgeoning above-ground economy, employing more people productively in it, must have drawn at least some of its strength from the black market, or underground economy, that existed during wartime.

In 1920, a total of 3,649 tax returns revealed incomes of $100,000 or more, and the federal government took in $321 million from total tax receipts. By 1928 the number of returns reporting an income of $100,000 or more had jumped to 16,000, and government tax revenues had soared to $714 million. It is apparent that, with lower tax rates and general increased prosperity, most people no longer had a great need to divert income to unproductive tax shelters or hide it illegally.

The Kennedy tax cuts of 1963–1964 produced similar results. Many had predicted that a 20 percent across-the-board reduction in personal income taxes would generate smaller revenues for the federal till. In fact, the government's income from taxes increased steadily throughout the 1960s, and unemployment dropped by nearly half between 1961 and 1969. Again, no one was measuring underground economic activities at the time, but we can assume that there is less of an incentive to hide income illegally during a period when the above-ground economy is expanding and the overall living standard is improving significantly.

Puerto Rico offers us another domestic example of what a lower tax rate can do for the visible, above-ground economy. When Governor Carlos Romero Barcelo of the New Progressive party was elected in 1976, he was advised by economist Arthur Laffer, one of the architects of President Reagan's economic program, to reduce Puerto Rican taxes sharply. Taking Laffer's advice, Romero Barcelo introduced a series of tax cuts totaling 15 percent between 1977 and 1980. By early 1980, the cumulative tax reductions had expanded the visible economy to a point where tax collections were running 13.5 percent ahead of the previous year.

"The things Laffer told us would happen are happening," said Governor Romero Barcelo in 1980. "In fact, he guaranteed it would happen. I'm sold that the Laffer theory is correct."

The Puerto Rican government is so sold, as a matter of fact, that he plans to initiate a new round of tax reductions amounting to 15 percent between 1981 and 1982. Puerto Rico's economy right now is as strong as it has ever been, and this period of economic expansion appears to be a direct result of the tax cut measures.

The recent history of tax *increases* is quite the opposite. When the maximum capital gains tax was doubled from 25 percent to 50 percent in 1969, government revenues from this source dropped substantially, and venture capital financing virtually dried up overnight. In 1978 the capital gains rate was lowered from a maximum of 50 percent to 28 percent, and tax revenues went up the following year. Venture capital formation likewise increased accordingly. If these domestic experiments with tax reductions and increases are any indication, it seems clear that tax cuts do lead to a more vibrant above-ground economy and, we assume, a diminished underground economy, while tax increases do quite the opposite.

The evidence from abroad seems to confirm these findings in the domestic arena. Two fledgling African nations, Ghana and the Ivory Coast, started out with essentially the same ethnic mix, natural resources, and per capita income in 1960. Politically and economically, however, they opted for completely divergent systems. Ghana imposed a punitive tax burden on its people, as well as heavy regulations on most economic activity. The Ivory Coast adopted a lower tax rate and a more open market system. Today, the Ivory Coast enjoys many times the per capita income of its struggling neighbor.

In Europe following World War II, Chancellor Konrad Adenauer and his economic minister, Ludwig Erhard, elected to follow a relatively laissez-faire economic program. Before Adenauer took office, the top tax rate in Germany was 95 percent on all incomes above $15,000. A thriving black market flourished in West Germany, beyond the reach of the tax agents. It was estimated that as much as 50 percent of German income went unreported and thus untaxed.

Starting in 1948, Adenauer inaugurated a series of sharp tax reductions, as well as tax incentives to encourage the people to save and invest their earnings. Ten years later, the top marginal tax rate had been lowered from 95 percent to 53 percent, and the income level at which the top rate went into effect was raised from $15,000 a year to $27,510. Since then, volumes have been written about Germany's postwar "economic miracle," which brought it from a nation in shambles in 1948 to a nation with the fourth largest gross national product in the world in 1978. Higher taxes imposed on the work force since that time have given Germany a larger underground economy proportionately than exists in the United States, but it is still far smaller than the enormous black market of the pre-Adenauer years.

Japan, too, is a case in point. During the initial occupation period following the war, Japan was saddled with extremely high progressive income tax rates, high corporate and excess-profits taxes, near confiscation of wealth, and a proliferation of sales and excise taxes. Accordingly, the tax-payment and tax-collection system had virtually broken down by 1949, dozens of businesses were failing every day, and underground economic activities in Japan had reached unmanageable proportions.

At the invitation of General Douglas MacArthur, a group of tax specialists headed by Professor Carl Shoup of Columbia University visited Japan to study the situation. Their first recommendation was a drastic reduction in tax rates and a corresponding increase in exemptions. The top bracket was immediately lowered from 85 to 55 percent, the personal exemption was raised from 15,000 to 24,000 yen, and a tax credit was allowed for dependents. The Shoup Mission, as the group was known, also introduced a depreciation schedule for Japanese business, reduced the corporate tax rate, and elminiated the excess-profits tax. Today, Japan enjoys the third largest GNP in the world, government tax revenues have steadily increased as taxes have been lowered even more between 1954 and 1974, and, as best as can be determined, the Japanese underground economy has not been a significant problem since the early years of the American occupation.

And then there is Hong Kong. Even more than the United States, Hong Kong is perhaps the greatest free market success story in history. Here is a city-country with a population density of 400,000 people per square mile, a total of 4.5 million human beings jammed into less than fifty of its four hundred square miles, a veritable human anthill. If this congestion weren't enough of a drawback, the colony must import 85 percent of its food, most of its raw materials, and all of its capital equipment.

If ever a social doomsday prophet wanted to invent a blueprint for starvation and misery, he could have done no better than conjure the specter of Hong Kong. And yet, Hong Kong not only manages to survive, it actually prospers under all this apparent adversity.

Between 1948 and 1977, per capita income in Hong Kong soared from $180 to $2,600 a year. Between 1960 and 1976, real GNP increased by 6.4 percent annually compared with 3.3 percent in West Germany and 2.4 percent a year in the United States.

When we look at the existing economic system in Hong Kong we see one of the freest market structures on the planet, as well as one of the lowest tax rates anywhere. The maximum tax on all profits is 17 percent, while the maximum tax on individual incomes is 15 percent. Economist Alvin Rabushka sums up the Hong Kong phenomenon this way: "Hong Kong has, to my knowledge, the lowest standard rate of tax on earnings and profits of any industrial state . . . a narrow tax base and low standard rates of direct taxation facilitate rapid economic growth which generates high and ever-increasing tax yields. These revenues, in turn, finance an extremely ambitious program of public expenditure on housing, education, health, and welfare services, and on other forms of social and community services, with virtually no need to resort to loan financing."

There is no need of a large underground economy in Hong Kong. Hong Kong, you see, simply legalized its underground economy and turned it into its official economy by adopting the lowest tax rates in the industrialized world. Hong Kong is perhaps the only place on earth where economic acts between consenting adults (and minors for that matter) go unpunished.

All these historical precedents are no guarantee that the latest round of tax cuts in the United States, initiated by the Reagan administration, will eliminate or significantly reduce the $700 billion underground economy. There is no question, however, that the basic thrust of the Reagan administration is to make capitalism respectable again. The profit motive has come into disrepute in recent years, and it has been discouraged accordingly with outlandishly high taxes on individuals and businesses. The new tax cuts, together with a philosophical tone that says that profits are good for all of us, should serve to direct more and more economic activity into the official, above-ground economy during the years ahead. Just how successful Reagan is in curtailing underground economic activities will depend on how committed he is to maintaining a steady course of action. If he continues to pursue a lower-tax, pro–free market policy, he has a good chance of creating an American economic miracle of sorts during his first term in office.

The United States still has a long way to go before it becomes a gargantuan, more orderly Hong Kong. But, for the moment at least, we have taken a small step in that direction.

In the next chapter we'll look at some measures you can take to reduce your own tax burden and win your personal rebellion against high taxes.

CHAPTER SIX

How to Profit Legally in the Underground Economy

Automatic Reductions—The Tax Cuts at Work

If you want to run off and join Lucille Moran and her army of non-filers, Irwin Schiff and the Fifth Amendment protesters, the Reverend Kirby Hensley and his Universal Life Church, or Mike Oliver and his tax-free utopia on some distant atoll, you are free to do so at your own risk. I am not about to advise anyone to take a course of action that could result not only in a hefty fine but perhaps in a jail sentence as well. It is up to you to assume that risk on your own if you are so inclined.

However, there are now plenty of legal methods of reducing your personal tax burden if you take the time to find out what they are. In the past, most of the tax shelters and loopholes in the tax law existed primarily for the wealthy. Those with incomes well up in six and seven figures were able, with the help of high-priced professional advisers, to avoid paying taxes altogether in some instances. Now, thanks to the Economic Recovery Tax Act of 1981, many tax-reduc-

129

ing investment incentives have been created for middle-income earners as well.

To begin with, everyone's personal income taxes will automatically be reduced by about 23 percent during the next few years. You don't have to do anything to take advantage of this tax cut; the new tax schedules will result in lower withholding taxes on your salaries in the years ahead. Also, beginning in 1985, your personal tax bracket will be indexed to inflation, again automatically, reducing your taxes even further as the rate of inflation at the time is taken into consideration.

Other automatic reductions in the tax schedules lower taxes for married couples with both parties working, lower taxes on long-term capital gains, lower taxes on commodities-trading profits, give people selling a principal residence up to twenty-four months to reinvest the profit in a new home without paying taxes on it, and increase the one-time exclusion from $100,000 to $125,000 for those fifty-five years of age and older who sell their principal residence. Again, you do not have to do anything special to take advantage of these cuts, except to hire a competent tax preparer who is familiar with the new rates.

Aside from these *scheduled* tax cuts, however, others are available to those who take the steps necessary to benefit from them. The advice that follows will be of interest primarily to single people earning over $18,200 in net taxable income in 1982, and married couples with at least $29,900 net taxable income for the same year. Those with lower incomes will not benefit as much from the financial advice I am about to give.

Three Basic Steps—IRA Accounts, All Savers Certificates, and Utilities Dividend Reinvestment

Let's look first at someone, married or single, who is in a 40 percent tax bracket in 1982. You are a salaried employee with a pension plan at work. You own your home and have $40,000 invested in a money market fund paying 17 percent a year in dividends.

$40,000 × 17% = $6,800 annually in taxable dividends. At your 40 percent bracket rate, $2,720 of this amount will go to Uncle Sam in taxes. You are left with $4,080 after taxes, or a net return of 10.2 percent of your investment.

Thanks to the Economic Recovery Tax Act of 1981, there are steps you should be taking now, before the end of 1982, to reduce your tax burden for the year.

To begin with, starting in 1982, you are for the first time permitted to open up a separate Individual Retirement Account (IRA) in addition to your company pension plan. Under the new law, every individual can contribute 100 percent of his or her income up to a maximum of $2,000 a year in an IRA. An individual with a nonworking spouse can contribute up to $250 a year in an IRA for the unemployed partner.

So, a single individual taxpayer should immediately remove $2,000 from the money market fund and invest this amount in an IRA. The tax savings here comes to $800, since the $2,000 contribution is deductible from ordinary income, and would have been taxable at your 40-percent-bracket rate. In addition, the profit from the investment is tax-deferred until you retire. Assuming that you invested this $2,000 in a money market fund paying 17 percent a year, the $340 a year you earn from this investment will not be subject to current taxes. Had the money not been reinvested in an IRA, you would have owed the government $136 in taxes on these dividends ($340 × 40% =$136). The total tax savings for an individual opening an IRA under the new law comes to $936 ($800 + $136 = $936).

The figures for a married couple with both partners working are even better. A husband and wife can each open an IRA for a total contribution of $4,000, resulting in a tax saving of $1,600. The $680 income generated by the investments will likewise save you another $272 in taxes, for an overall tax saving of $1,872.

Step 1: Open up an IRA before 1982 runs out.

Another feature of the new tax law is the creation of the All Savers Certificate, which will be available until December 31, 1982. The All Savers Certificate is a new investment vehicle designed to provide individual taxpayers with up to $1,000 in tax-free income and married couples a maximum of $2,000. This is a one-time, lifetime exclusion and is scheduled to expire after 1982, so you will have to act quickly to take advantage of it.

With an All Savers Certificate, you must tie your money up for one year. At the end of this period, you will get back your principal plus the tax-free interest, which will be pegged at 70 percent of the going rate for one-year Treasury bills. At this writing the yield on one-year Treasury bills is a bit over 17 percent which means the banks are paying a shade more than 12 percent for the All Savers investment.

With these numbers in effect, an individual taxpayer should remove $8,330 from the money market fund and invest this amount in the All Savers one-year obligation for a tax-free yield of $1,000. With a taxable return of 17 percent in the money market fund, you are left with only about $850 after taxes at your 40 percent bracket rate ($8,330 × 17% = $1,416 — $566 in taxes = $850). You can see that the tax saving here for an individual taxpayer is $150.

A married couple should double this investment to $16,660 in an All Savers Certificate. This will generate $2,000 in tax-free income for a total tax break of $300, twice as much as that for the single taxpayer. Again, we are talking about those of you in a 40 percent tax bracket with the prevailing interest rates at the time I am writing this. Changes in interest rates will, of course, change the numbers around, but the tax benefits will still be there. As a general rule, no one in a bracket lower than 30 percent should contemplate buying an All Savers Certificate, while those in brackets higher than 40 percent will benefit even more than these figures allow.

Step 2: Buy an All Savers Certificate while you still can.

A provision in the new tax law overlooked by many analysts is one permitting shareholders of public utilities to reinvest their dividends into additional shares and convert taxable cash dividends into nontaxable stock dividends. From 1982 through the end of 1985, you can have the utilities reinvest your dividends in new stock and exclude up to $750 a year in income for individual taxpayers and up to $1,500 annually if you are married and filing jointly. When you sell your stock, providing you have held the shares for over a year, the stock dividends will be taxed at a capital gains rate up to a maximum of 20 percent. Those of you in the 40 percent bracket, which we have been using for purposes of illustration here, will be taxed a long-term capital gains rate of 16 percent.

In effect, you will pay no taxes whatsoever on utility stock dividends through the end of 1985 if you do not sell them, and you will be converting ordinary income (taxable at 40 percent) into long-term capital gains (taxable at 16 percent) for stock dividends you sell after a one-year period.

At this writing, electric utility stocks are yielding about 15 percent. Using this figure, individual taxpayers should remove $5,000 from the money market fund and buy qualified electric utility stocks, requesting that the cash dividends be reinvested in additional shares. This realignment of your financial reserves will generate $750 a year in tax-free income, whereas previously it was earning $850 annually in taxable income, leaving you with $510 after taxes ($5,000 × 17% = $850 − $340 in taxes = $510). The saving here for individual taxpayers is $240.

Married couples are able to double up again and invest $10,000 in electric utilities, generating $1,500 a year in tax-free stock dividends. Their savings after taxes will be twice as much, or $480.

Step 3: Be sure to take advantage of the exclusion for the dividend reinvestment provision.

These three steps are basic and should be utilized by everyone looking to profit from the tax rebellion. Once you have taken them, you will have altered your financial situation in the following way:

OLD INVESTMENT

Money market fund: $40,000
Yield: 17 percent
Income: $6,800 taxable income

NEW INVESTMENTS

Individual

IRA:	$2,000
Tax saving:	$ 936
All Savers?	$8,330
Tax saving:	$ 150
Utilities:	$5,000
Tax saving:	$ 240
Total tax saving:	$1,326

Balance of investment to be discussed below.

Married Couple

IRA:	$ 4,000
Tax saving:	$ 1,872
All Savers?	$16,660
Tax saving:	$ 300
Utilities:	$10,000
Tax saving:	$ 480
Total tax saving:	$ 2,652

Balance of investment to be discussed below.

Other Options—Some Sample Portfolios

By following Steps 1, 2, and 3, the individual tax-payer has removed $15,330 from the money market fund and reinvested it in a way that will save a total of $1,326 in taxes, while the married couple reinvested $30,660 to save itself $2,652. This leaves the individual with approximately $25,000 to invest and the couple with about $10,000.

Let's take a look at some sample portfolios ranging from $10,000 to $25,000 in discretionary cash. As I mentioned at the beginning of this chapter, I am assuming that you own your home. If you do not, I suggest that you buy either a principal residence or a weekend retreat before embarking on Steps 1, 2, and 3. Homeownership is still the best tax shelter of all as long as the government permits us to deduct mortgage interest payments from our ordinary income. If the day ever arrives when this policy is changed, it will be time to take a new look at the situation.

What follows will be of interest to those of you who own a home, have realigned your finances according to the steps I have just outlined, and are still left with between $10,000 and $25,000 in discretionary cash. I will set up some sample portfolios below to show you how you can best win your personal tax rebellion.

$10,000

Money market fund: $5,000
Tax shelter: $5,000

You should always keep about $5,000 liquid cash ready for whatever emergencies may arise. The best place to park cash reserves is in a money market fund, particularly one providing check-writing and credit card privileges, so that you can withdraw whatever amound you need on a moment's notice. Money market funds offer much higher yields than you can get from a day-to-day savings account in a bank, and they are extremely safe in most instances.

The rest of your money should be invested in a limited partnership in either an oil- and gas-drilling program or a residential real estate deal. The major brokerage firms all offer middle-income investors oil and gas shelters which you can get into for as little as $5,000.

These programs fall into three broad categories: exploratory, developmental, and combination. In the first case, the greatest amount of risk is involved, since the general partners will be drilling in areas where there are no known gas or oil reserves. If they get lucky and strike a bonanza, you stand to make a lot of money from tax-sheltered oil royalties for as long as the wells continue to pay off. If, on the other hand, they come up dry, you can lose your entire investment.

Developmental programs are less risky, since the wells are being sunk in areas where producing wells already exist. Your chances of losing your investment are very slim, and you are more than likely to receive a good, tax-sheltered cash return on your money. But there is almost no chance that you are going to get rich in a developmental program, since the amount of oil and gas in the ground is pretty well determined beforehand.

Combination programs are, as the name implies, a mixture of the first two. They involve a modest amount of risk with an outside chance of striking a rich reserve somewhere.

The amount of money you invest in an oil and gas limited partnership also provides you with a deduction from your income. In some cases, you may be able to deduct the full amount from your taxable income: in others the write-off might be 40 to 50 percent of the investment. Usually, the earlier in the year that you invest in a tax shelter, the greater the deduction. Accordingly, you should start shopping around in the spring of the year and not wait until the fall or early winter, when there is always a mad scramble for whatever deals are left.

If you are fortunate enough to find a good program with a 100 percent deduction, those of you in the 40 percent tax bracket will save $2,000 in taxes for the year, since that is the amount you would have had to pay Uncle Sam had you invested the money elsewhere. In reality then, you only have $3,000 at risk; the federal government is your partner for the balance of the investment. Naturally, the higher your tax bracket, the greater the tax benefit. Those of you falling significantly below 40 percent should not contemplate this type of program at all.

A limited partnership in a real estate tax shelter works a bit differently. I suggest getting into a residential shelter rather than a commercial real estate deal because, under the new tax law, residential real estate benefits more than commercial property does from the changes in depreciation rules. Most of the major financial firms sell limited partnerships in garden apartment complexes and high-rise apartment houses, many of them located in the growing Sun Belt, to the investing public.

When you buy into a real estate shelter, there are three basic tax advantages to look for. The first one is the write-off you get on your investment. This can be a straight deduction from your income, as in the case of an oil and gas shelter, or an investment tax credit, which is even better. The second advantage is immediate tax-sheltered cash flow from the rents, which are passed along to the limited partners. Finally, there is the prospect of a substantial capital gain several years down the road when the properties are sold, and the profits are shared by the limited partners who will be taxed at a long-term capital gains rate at the end.

It is up to you to decide how much risk you are willing to live with when you put money into a tax shelter. An exploratory oil and gas program can make you rich, but it also involves the highest degree of risk. Developmental and real estate shelters can provide you with a decent economic return, and the risk is moderate. The greatest potential rewards go to those who are willing to assume the risk, and that is just as it should be.

Whatever the case, the shelters I have just described provide you with an opportunity to keep your taxes to a minimum, and you ought to look into them.

$15,000

Money market fund:	$5,000
Tax shelter:	$5,000
Annuity:	$5,000

A tax-deferred annuity is an absolutely risk-free investment marketed by insurance companies and brokerage firms. Unlike a municipal bond, the principal never fluctuates and you will never receive less than the principal amount you invested should you ever decide you want to liquidate the investment and get your money back.

When you invest money in an annuity, the interest is ordinarily guaranteed for the first year, while a lower rate is guaranteed after the first year if interest rates fall in the future. At this writing, it is possible to buy an annuity with a 15½ percent gurantee for the first twelve months, and a minimum guarantee of 14¼ percent thereafter. The interest is compounded annually, and it accrues, tax-deferred, until you decide to draw out the interest. At that time, you will have to pay tax on it.

Another advantage of annuities is that, unlike your other assets, they are not subject to probate when you die. The proceeds pass immediately to your beneficiary. On the negative side, there is sometimes a penalty if you draw out more than 6 percent of the accumulated amount in any one year. Some annuities have a sliding scale so that you are free to liquidate the entire amount without penalty after the first six years. It pays to shop around and find out which ones have the best all-around features for you.

Using the lower rate mentioned above (14¼ percent), your money will double every five years. Fifty thousand dollars invested today will be worth $100,-000 in five years, $200,000 in ten years, $400,000 in fifteen years, and $800,000 twenty years from now. This is a nice way to build up equity for your retirement without taking any risk at all, and enjoy significant tax advantages while you are doing it.

$20,000

Money market fund:	$5,000
Tax shelter:	$5,000
Annuity:	$5,000
Municipal bonds:	$5,000

Municipal bonds, which are exempt from federal income taxes in all cases and from state and local taxes as well if they are issued within the state you reside in, are the traditional investment vehicle for those looking for tax-free income. Again, you should not buy them at all if you are in significantly less than a 40 percent tax bracket, since you can do better elsewhere. Tax-free yields of 13 percent are available as I am writing this, which means that those of you in a 40 percent bracket need a taxable yield of 22 percent to do as well after taxes.

Unlike annuities, tax-free bonds involve a degree of risk. If the municipality that issues them founders upon financial shoals, as was the case with New York City a few years back, your interest and principal can be in jeopardy, for a while at least. Also, if you buy them at the wrong time, the value of the bonds can decline in value over time.

As it turned out, almost any time before the fall of 1981 was the wrong time to buy bonds of any kind. Just about every bond issued before that time has lost value, in some cases 50 percent or more of face value. As interest rates soared for a solid year following the election of 1980, bonds and other fixed-income investments started to plummet. That is the nature of the beast. Bonds fluctuate in value counter to the direction of interest rates.

But bonds can be an extremely attractive vehicle when interest rates are starting to fall again. This being the case in November 1981, municipal bonds offered a rare opportunity to lock in high tax-free income plus substantial capital gain. Be careful about buying bonds with very long-term maturities, however. If you guess wrong about the future direction of interest rates, you will be stuck with hefty losses for years before you get even again. Keep your maturities relatively short, and you will reduce your risk to a minimum.

$25,000

Money market fund:	$5,000
Tax shelter:	$5,000
Annuity:	$5,000
Municipal bonds:	$5,000
Gifts:	$5,000

Prior to the Economic Recovery Tax Act of 1981, parents were limited in the amount they could transfer to their children without paying taxes on the income; the maximum was $6,000 a year. Now the ceiling has been raised to $10,000 for each parent, or a maximum total of $20,000 annually for each child.

If you have children under eighteen years of age who will be heading for college, consider transferring assets into a custodian account for them now. The interest and dividends earned in a custodian account will not be taxable, since your children do not have enough income to qualify for taxes. Since this money is earmarked for their education anyway, you might as well take advantage of all the available tax benefits.

The same holds true for an aging relative, without appreciable income, whom you are supporting. You cannot set up a custodian account in this case since the relative is over eighteen, but you can establish a reversionary trust in which the untaxed income is used to provide for your relative's welfare, and the money reverts to you upon his or her death. By keeping this money in your own name, the profits are being taxed away at your bracket rate even though they are being used for someone else's benefit.

For Those Who Don't Mind a Little Risk

So far we have seen how those of you with fairly substantial assets can reorganize your finances in such a way that you will pay little or no taxes on them. With all these legal loopholes available for the middle-income taxpayer, it really doesn't make any sense to get involved in any of the illegal tax rebellion schemes discussed earlier in this book. Indeed, the only taxable investment of all those discussed in this chapter is the liquid cash kept in the money market fund, and even this could be tax-sheltered by putting it in a tax-free money fund instead, which pays lower interest than the ordinary funds. Those of you who are fortunate enough to have assets in excess of the amounts covered here can also avoid taxes by increasing the amounts allocated to tax shelters, annuities, municipal bonds, and tax-excluded gifts. Virtually any amount can be invested in shelters and other tax-advantaged vehicles.

This strategy is for those of you whose primary goal is to avoid taxes without assuming any great degree of risk. It is a *legal tax-avoidance* program. There is little in it that will turn you into a millionaire overnight, unless you happen to get lucky on an oil and gas deal, but it is a means of engaging in your personal tax revolt without running afoul of the IRS.

If you have some gambling blood in you, however, and you don't mind risking some of your hard-earned dollars in an attempt to make some big money, there is much in the new tax law to benefit the free-wheeling trader. To begin with, the maximum tax on all long-term capital gains is now 20 percent, which means the most Uncle Sam can confiscate from your winnings is one dollar out of five.

For tax purposes, the long-term holding period is still one year and a day. Anything sold for a profit that was held for at least one year and a day is a long-term gain. Since 60 percent of a long-term gain is excluded from taxes, the remaining 40 percent will be taxed at your bracket rate. The capital gains rate for those of you in a 40 percent tax bracket is 16 percent (40 percent of the profit × 40 percent bracket rate = 16 percent). So, if you have $1,000 in long-term winnings, you only have to turn over $160 in taxes to the IRS. Short-term gains are considered ordinary income, and taxed accordingly at your full bracket rate.

Another provision of the tax law limits the tax on profits in commodities accounts to a maximum of 32 percent. Regardless of how long you hold a commodity position, 60 percent of the gain is regarded as long-term for tax purposes, and 40 percent is considered short-term. Therefore, if you are in a 50 percent bracket, the most tax you can pay is 20 percent of the long-term portion (20% × 60% = 12%) and 50 percent of the short-term portion (50% × 40% = 20%), or a maximum of 32 percent (12% + 20% = 32%). In a 40 percent tax bracket, your tax on commodity trading profits will come to 25.6 percent (I'll let you do the math yourself in this case; if you can't figure it out, you shouldn't be trading commodities).

If you have the stomach for it, then, if your blood is pounding through your veins with a mania to turn your $40,000 stake in life into $100,000, $250,000, who knows, maybe a million, then put up your money and place your bet secure in the knowledge that your government will leave you with the lion's share of your profits after taxes.

If gambling is your game, and you are inclined to take your shot at getting rich, I would recommend forgetting about the annuity and the municipal bonds, and instead dividing this money equally between a managed commodities account and the stock market. Don't try trading commodities yourself unless you are a seasoned trader. The professionals, who earn a living at it year after year, will eat you alive in short order. Find a major brokerage firm or a reputable commodities house, and ask to see their track record on managed commodities accounts. Select the one that looks the most promising, invest your funds, then sit back prepared to wait a year and a half or so to see the results. You will either be wiped out or substantially ahead within two years.

As far as stocks are concerned, the big money to be made in the years ahead will be on the takeover stocks. Select a portfolio of good-quality stocks that are potential takeover targets, and forget about it for at least a year. If I am right and the stock market is strong during this period, you will wind up making money on your stocks. If you are really lucky, you could wind up catching lightning in a bottle and having one of your stocks acquired by another firm at several times your purchase price. Below is a list of recommended stocks for long-term investment as well as takeover potential:

Corporation	Current price	Potential take-over price
E. F. Hutton	36	80
Amerada Hess	26	75
Occidental Petroleum	24	75
Ashland Oil	28	70
Diamond Shamrock	27	70
Pittston	24	55
Louisiana Land	27	60
Mesa Petroleum	20	55
Cities Service	38	80
Tosco	20	60
Kaneb	21	60
Donaldson, Lufkin	10	30
Moseley Hallgarten	3	12
A. G. Edwards	22	45

Some Last-Minute Reminders

In addition to the programs we have talked about in this chapter, you should be aware of a few other legal techniques that can help reduce your tax bill.

If it is possible, it will pay you to defer as much income as you can until next year, and generate deductions or losses for the current tax year. Since the tax rate will be reduced again in 1983, with the full benefit of the Economic Recovery Tax Act of 1981 being felt in 1984, your income will automatically be taxed at a lower rate in the years ahead. Then, with indexing going into effect in 1985, your tax brackets will be lowered each year according to the inflation rate. Unless the government alters these provisions in the tax act, you will save money by deferring income for as long as you can.

Second, do not allow your investment losses to become long-term. If you have a loss on a stock or bond that you purchased within the past twelve months, sell it while it is still a short-term loss and reinvest the money into something similar. This is known as swapping for tax purposes, and the concept is the same whether you are doing a stock or a bond swap. Short-term losses are 100 percent deductible from ordinary income, while you can take off only fifty cents on the dollar for a long-term loss.

For example, let's say you bought 20 U.S. Treasury bonds with a 7¼ percent coupon maturing in 1992 for a price of $750 a bond, or $15,000,less than a year ago. Today the bond is trading for $630. By selling it for a total of $12,600, you will have a $2,400 deduction from your income for the current tax year. If you want to keep the money in a similar investment, you can simultaneously buy the U.S. Treasury 7⅞ percent bonds of 1993. which are selling for approximately the same price. You will have maintained essentially the same investment and actually increased your annual income a bit by extending your maturity a year while generating a deduction for yourself. As long as two out of the three basic bond features are different, your swap is legal. In this instance, the coupon rate and maturity date of the new bond are different from the old one, and the issuing institution (the U.S. Treasury) is the same.

In the case of selling a stock for a short-term loss, the law says that for the loss to be recognized you must wait at least thirty-one days before buying the stock back. Another way of doing it is to buy an equal amount of stock first at the lower price, then wait at least thirty-one days before selling your original shares for a loss. For example, we'll assume you bought 100 shares of RCA eight months ago for $30 a share. Today the stock has fallen to $20. You can either sell the RCA for a tax loss now and wait thirty-one days before buying it back, or buy another 100 shares of RCA first and sell the original 100 shares thirty-one days later for a tax loss.

The danger with this strategy, of course, is that the price of the shares can change dramatically during this waiting period. You could sell your stock for a ten-point loss today, then end up paying six points more for it when you buy it back.

One way to get around this problem is to sell your stock today and buy another similar stock at the same time. If you were selling U.S. Steel for a loss you could immediately reinvest the proceeds into Bethlehem Steel or Republic Steel. Westinghouse would be a good swap substitute for RCA, Exxon for Mobil, Diamond Shamrock for Pittston, and so on. Usually you will want to look for an equally good company within the same industry. There is no guarantee that all stocks within the same industry will fluctuate in tandem, but, then again, if you weren't willing to take some element of risk you wouldn't be in the stock market in the first place.

Third, if you are selling stock for a *short-term profit*, consider selling it *short against the box* in order to defer the gain until next year, when you will be taxed at a lower rate. Let's say that you have a ten-point profit on a stock and you are afraid you will lose it if you hang on to it until next year. You can sell it now to lock in your profit, and deliver the shares you sold after January 1 to completely close out the sale. For tax purposes, the gain becomes effective at the time you close out the short sale, and the profit will be taxed at a lower marginal bracket rate.

A variation of this strategy is to buy a put on your stock to lock in a short-term gain, and defer the taxes to the following year. You would do this instead of selling short against the box if you thought your stock had a chance of moving even higher. If, for example, you bought 100 shares of Mobil at 25 and saw it run to 40 a short time later, you could buy a put with a strike price of 40 expiring in the following year. The put would cost approximately two points, or $200. If Mobil continues to move up after you buy the put, you will be able to participate in the advance, since you still own the stock. But if it drops back down below 40, you would then exercise your put before it expires, thereby guaranteeing yourself a sale price of $40 a share minus the cost of the put. In any event, the profit is locked in and is not subject to tax until the next year.

For additional information on how to profit the most from the taxpayer's revolt, write to me and enclose a stamped, self-addressed envelope:

Jerome Tuccille
% Collier Associates
280 Madison Avenue
New York, N.Y. 10016

The End is Nowhere in Sight

And still, the revolution continues.

On April 30, 1981, the New York State Court of Appeals ruled that the so-called mail-order ministers of the Town of Hardenburgh could not get tax exemptions for their property unless it was held exclusively for church use.

Case closed?

Hardly. In a companion ruling, the same court said that the State Board of Equalization and Assessment did not have the power to tax this property without proper hearings and procedural safeguards.

The Town of Hardenburgh, New York, boasts 236 citizens. Of this number, 200 became ordained ministers in the Reverend Kirby Hensley's Universal Life Church based in Modesto, California, and filed for property tax exemptions. Homeowners in nearby towns in Ulster County quickly followed their example.

A suit was brought against the newly ordained ministers by state officials, and it worked its way up through the court system from 1977 to 1981, with both sides claiming victory along the way. At various times, the State Board of Equalization and Assessment ordered town officials to restore the homes to the tax rolls while local assessors, siding with the homeowners, maintained that the law did not require them to do so. When legislative guidelines were imposed on January 1, 1979, limiting religious tax exemptions to property "held in trust by a clergyman or minister of a religious denomination for the benefit of the members" of the church, the lawyer for the town, Stephen Oppenheim, said that he would appeal this decision to the Supreme Court. "The First Amendment does not permit this type of change in statutes regarding religion," said Oppenheim.

The latest ruling, passed down by the New York State Court of Appeals in 1981, still leaves the matter up in the air. The state took the position that the court clearly ordered the homes in Ulster County restored to the tax rolls, while town officials refused to comply pending "proper hearings and procedural safeguards."

Meanwhile, in Boston, Mayor Kevin White predicted that the citizenry would "go into a rage" when the full impact of Proposition 2½ finally hit them in July 1981, when it was due to go into effect. The mayor was correct. The rage of the people, however, instead of being directed at the state legislature or the city council, as he had predicted, was focused primarily on himself.

"The problem is not 2½, the problem is Emperor White," said James P. Kelley, president of the South Boston Information Center, while addressing an enthusiastic crowd in front of City Hall. His audience, composed primarily of laid-off policemen and firefighters, members of various neighborhood organizations, and their sympathizers, responded with chants of "Recall! Recall!" and demanded that the mayor be removed from office.

A statewide poll taken in the spring of 1981 indicated that more than half of the population thought that Mayor White had implemented Proposition 2½ in a way designed to make it unworkable. Two-thirds of the people polled in Boston alone claimed that White had fired policemen, firemen, and other vital employees deliberately, in an attempt to make the public think 2½ was against their best interests. Critics of the mayor had been accusing him for a long time of living luxuriously at the public's expense and using tax money to build and maintain his own political machine. His personal staff was estimated to number as many as three thousand of a total of fourteen thousand city employees.

Michael Donovan, a spokesman for the mayor, defended his boss by stating, "This is one of those peculiar instances when strengths turn against you. People elected him mayor because he is perceived as a strong manager. Now that political and financial problems converge, people blame him for the present situation even though he is not responsible for it."

The battle on this front, it seems, has only just begun.

And in Washington, D.C., the Reagan administration ordered the IRS to comply with key sections of the Fair Debt Collection Practices Act. Accordingly, the agency issued new guidelines for its agents to follow in the future.

Among them: IRS agents may not communicate with you at a time or place that is inconvenient for you, or at your place of employment if you ask them not to. As a general guide, the hours between 8:00 A.M. and 9:00 P.M. are considered to be reasonable.

Agents must also deal directly with your attorney if they know you have one.

The new IRS guidelines remind agents that they may not harass taxpayers, use threats of violence, obscene or profane language, or make abusive or annoying phone calls.

According to Philip P. Storrer, an accounting professor at California State University at Hayward, the latest IRS guidelines give the taxpayer the authority to settle collection problems in a "more businesslike and predictable fashion."

A Final Word From the IRS

It will be a long time before we hear the final word on this subject, but perhaps the last word here should come from Roscoe Egger, commissioner of the IRS. Unlike Jerome Kurtz, who preceded him, Egger is regarded as a political conservative who sympathizes with the philosophy of the current administration in Washington. He is a former partner in the accounting firm of Price Waterhouse & Co., and he has been a tax specialist throughout his working life. James C. Miller III, director of regulation for the Office of Management and Budget and executive director of George Bush's Task Force on Regulatory Relief, declared in May 1981, "Half the government's paperwork is generated by IRS. Roscoe is a great administrator and is going to do wonderful things."

Echoing this line, Egger said that one of his main priorities would be to look "at every single thing we ask for in the way of information" in an effort to cut back on IRS paperwork. As long as the Reagan administration remains opposed to further IRS harassment of the American taxpayer, Egger is expected to go along. One area in which he will get tougher in the years ahead, however, is the one involving "abusive" tax shelters, which he admits are a pet peeve of his. He believes that the penalties for the use of questionable tax shelters are too light, and he intends to make appropriate changes.

"One of the recommendations I've already made," he said during an interview with *Barron's* in 1981, "is to increase the rate of interest we charge on deficiencies for illegal tax shelters, so that taxpayers won't be encouraged to drag their feet closing cases."

Specifically, The Economic Recovery Tax Act of 1981 bans commodity straddles as a way of deferring taxes, a system which, ironically enough, was developed by Merrill Lynch, whose former chairman, Donald Regan, is now secretary of the treasury and Egger's boss. Regan defended the practice vigorously over the years as a sound economic strategy, but it is now illegal.

Egger warned that all returns employing tax shelters of any kind would be selected more frequently for general audit, and he reiterated his policy of looking at gross income on a return before all the deductions come into play.

"We used to score returns just on adjusted income," he said. "But in tax shelters, you conceivably could have a return with a gross income of $200,000 and a $180,000 offset, so we'd be scoring this as a $20,000 return. Now we score them on gross income, as well as adjusted gross income."

On the subject of the IRS's dreaded Taxpayer Compliance Measurement Program (TCMP), in which the agency randomly selects fifty thousand returns for an intensive, detailed audit, Egger had this to say. "This is a very intensive audit program and is intended to develop statistics on a whole variety of things.

It's research as well as audit. And then we take the physical data developed in these samplings and manipulate that data to produce relationships between, say, a percentage of deduction for this against gross income and just a whole long list of formula items. And then, if on a cumulative basis over a long time, it fits into a pattern, we use those characteristics as a means of selecting returns for audit."

In 1981, a woman named Susan Long brought a suit against the IRS and won a decision from a federal court ordering the agency to turn over the raw data obtained from the TCMP audits under the Freedom of Information Act. IRS appealed this decision to the Ninth Circuit Court of Appeals and lost. The appeals court ordered IRS to turn over its raw data "forthwith." Egger maintained that he would seek federal legislation to protect this information, and, in September 1981, the government ruled in the IRS's favor. Now it is Long who is appealing.

"If we have to disclose our selection criteria, it would be a fairly simple thing for anybody to frustrate the program. And with 95 million returns to worry about, we cannot possibly do it by hand."

Egger took a more conciliatory attitude on the subject of taxing fringe benefits. Jimmy Carter had criticized businessmen who deduct all those "three martini lunches" as business expenses, and he had ordered Jerome Kurtz to crack down on them. But Egger, a man who had perhaps indulged in a few of his own when he was with Price Waterhouse, was not nearly as critical. "We intend to use a rule of reason in this area because you can't tax every item that would be considered a fringe," he said wryly.

The underground economy, however, was one area that got Egger's blood flowing a bit more rapidly. He estimated that the IRS lost about $25 billion a year in taxes on unreported income. While he had no expectation of recovering all of it, he hoped to make it more difficult to hide income from Uncle Sam by initiating certain changes. One such change would be to require businessmen to file 1099 forms on fees paid to independent contractors. Until now, IRS had to rely on the integrity of freelancers to voluntarily declare this income when making out their returns. Egger, if he gets his way, will impose stiff penalties on businesses that fail to file the 1099s.

As far as the collection of delinquent taxes is concerned, Commissioner Egger hopes to improve the IRS's image as a bully, without regard for the rights and privacy of American citizens. According to him, there will be no more forcible entry to seize property, and no more liens on $100,000 houses to satisfy $2,000 tax bills. He expressed anguish over the incident I described earlier, involving the couple in Alaska who locked themselves inside their Volkswagen as IRS agents smashed the windows in with nightsticks.

"I've had complaints about individual circumstances, and each time we looked into it and followed it right up. With as many people as we have in the Internal Revenue Service, it would be impossible for me to say that occasionally some of them wouldn't use bad judgment . . . I'm looking at all our communications with people to see that we deal with them in the appropriate fashion; it's all part and parcel of trying to upgrade our image with the general public."

On October 1, 1981, the Equal Access to Justice Act went into effect. This law says that if any federal agency's ruling are successfully challenged in court, that agency must pay the court costs and legal fees of the plaintiff. Egger is unhappy with this statute on the grounds that "with anything as complex as the Internal Revenue Code . . . there can be honest differences of opinion." The IRS would be severely restricted, he said, if it has to pay the court costs of every case it loses.

Further restrictions on the IRS, however, are bound to bring smiles to the faces of the rest of the population, which feels it has been hounded and harassed by government long enough. Egger, with considerable nudging by the Reagan administration, apparently intends to add a dollop of honey to the vinegar approach to tax collection launched with a vengeance by his predecessor, Jerome Kurtz.

Much that happens in the future depends a great deal on the changes taking place in the nation's capital. The administration can defuse a lot of the revolutionary sentiment sweeping across the country by following through with the details of its own economic revolution. When all the budget cutting and tax cutting and deregulating take hold, the need of the American people to hide their income from the government will be greatly reduced.

But, until it all falls in place, the revolution will continue at an energetic pace.

ABOUT THE AUTHOR

JEROME TUCCILLE is Vice President/Investments with the brokerage house of Shearson/American Express. He is the author of several highly regarded financial books, including the recent *Dynamic Investing*, published by NAL Books, and *The New Tax Law and You*, available in a Signet edition.

Index

159